Blue Goat

The Life Changing Power of Being Yourself

Court Creeden

ISBN: 978-0-9994779-0-8

To you, the reader.

You can change your life to get the stuff you think you need or you can change the world because of who you are.

CONTENTS

Acknowledgments i

1 Chicken Nugget Pg 1

2 T.W.N.Y Pg 6

3 Blue Dot Pg 10

4 The Herd Pg 28

5 But Why? Pg 44

6 Tomorrow Pg 51

7 Well Rounded Pg 57

8 Check the Box Pg 66

9 GOOOOOAAAAL!!! Pg 74

10 This Is It? Pg 79

11 Sewer Grate Pg 86

12 Wrong Recipe Pg 93

13 Co-Pilot Pg 100

14 Golden Egg Pg 106

15 What If Pg 112

16 Yes, To You Pg 122

17 Dominos Pg 127

18 Main Attraction Pg 134

19 Solo Pg 138

20	Visit In The Night	Pg 148
21	There Is A Way Out?	Pg 154
22	What Do You Do?	Pg 161
23	Bungee Cord & Rope	Pg 169
24	One Degree	Pg 176
25	Snowflake	Pg 180
26	Blue Goat Life	Pg 184

ACKNOWLEDGMENTS

To all the special people that have been a part of the journey. All of the C's, E's, N's, S's, and my PF and MM families. To everyone who shared their truth, opened up their world, and changed my life by sharing their story.
To my everything, my LOM.

Editing by Margaret Diehl and Jeanne De Vita
Anna Smith and Chou Xiong at Hibiscus
Jamie Leigh Photography

1 CHICKEN NUGGET

What is the real goal?

When you think about your life, what is it that you hope for?

Most people you ask want enough money so they can do and have what they want, to work in a great job, to feel successful, and live with a sense of purpose. Yet it seems like everyone else can achieve those things rather than it happening to us.

Your neighbor has the brand-new car in the driveway, your co-worker gets the promotion and raise you were wanting, your sister seems to have the perfect marriage, you see pictures on Facebook of your high school friend living it up on their trip to Europe, and a stranger buys the dream home you are always doing virtual tours of on Zillow.

It seems like so many others are "living the dream" and enjoying everything that life has to offer.

That just isn't what is really going on.

Each day I spend hours and hours talking with people. From the girl starting her career in marketing, to the young couple preparing the nursery for their first baby. The parents who are trying so hard to help pay for their child's college, to the retirees doing their best to navigate the golden years of life. I've spent the better part of the last decade talking with people and helping them with their finances.

As an advisor, I've been given the opportunity to see what so many others haven't.

They've let me see behind the curtain. Your co-worker told me things they would never want anyone else to know. The "successful couple" opened the door to show me the skeletons in their closet. They've given me the unedited picture of what is really happening in their lives. I know the truth of what is going on with the people you spend time with and compare yourself to.

You only get to see the fresh, warm, golden brown chicken nugget.

I've been given the tour and shown what actually goes into it.

It's not what you think.

The life everyone wants you to see is not the one they are really living. You compare yourself to the delicious chicken nugget, but don't see how much stress, disappointment, frustration, time, energy, and fake stuff goes into making it. Regardless of how many zeroes are in their account, the issues are almost always the same.

What I've seen, heard, and experienced has changed my perspective on everything I thought I knew.

I've found that the lives that so many people live are far removed from what they really expect or want for themselves. Most people miss out on the life they could have, to live the life they think they are supposed to.

Our time is spent focused on keeping up with everyone else rather than focusing on what we want for ourselves. We are so consumed with whether the grass is greener everywhere else that we rarely pay attention to our own yard.

We are unfulfilled, more stressed, overwhelmed, and more worried than we ever want anyone else to know.

We have less love, joy, happiness, freedom, and less of the life we want. There has never been more opportunity, resources, technology, research, and ways to find ourselves, but we barely know who we are.

Yet we are all in the same place.

I can't tell you how many times I've been asked "*Am I the only one who is this stressed out?*", "*Are we the only ones who think parenting is hard as hell?*", "*Am I the only one who feels like I don't have it all together?*", "*Are we the only ones who feel like we can't keep up with everyone else?*", "*Does everyone else know what they are doing and I'm the only one who is trying to figure it all out?*". When you hear these questions day after day, month after month, and year after year, it isn't a coincidence.

We assume that everyone else is living the amazing life we can only dream of. Even worse, so many are giving up who they are and what really matters for all the wrong reasons. Not knowing that the people they compare themselves to are worrying and struggling to keep up with everyone else too. As a result, so many of us step into the great rat race, the never-ending cycle of trying to keep up with everyone else. Worrying if we are enough and have enough.

This isn't just about money; it is about how we look at our lives and the choices we make.

If you sat in the meetings and heard what I heard, your life might be different. You might look at your life through a different lens and with a new perspective. It's time you see what others are doing so you can stop worrying about everyone else and start focusing on yourself. It is time to begin a new conversation. With ourselves and with others. Not about what we want everyone else to think about us, what we hope they say, or what we hope they see us as.

It is time to remove the fancy wrapping, fake lighting, the smoke and mirrors.

To stop living based on what you think you are supposed to do, and show up as yourself.

To feel so grateful to be you, that you no longer want to be anyone else.

Blue Goat is a new perspective that was born out of the truth of what is happening in the lives of so many. It is about taking the real struggles that we face and seeing if there is a better way. About choosing to examine who we are to see if there is more to life and challenging others to do the same. What follows is my new view of the world based on what I've been told over the years. Each chapter represents an issue, topic, or aspect of life that so many appear to be working through.

Blue Goat is about looking deeper to see what really matters. Not what you think matters to everyone else, but what matters to you.

To get back the real version of you that may have been lost along the road to where you are now.

2 T.W.N.Y

Right now, you could be anywhere doing literally anything you want.

So many other books could be where this one is. Tens of thousands of other books could be in your hands right now. You could be watching the latest Netflix release, the game, the Real Housewives of somewhere, hanging out with friends, or working out at the gym, but you aren't. There is a message in this book that is meant for you. You may not believe it yet, but this book chose you.

Maybe a friend read *Blue Goat* and recommended it to you. That's happened to you countless times though. You've heard about great books you should read, movies you have to see, TV shows you can't miss, and amazing songs you have to download, but you didn't seek any of those things out. You didn't listen then.

Yet, here you are.

This book isn't in your hands because someone told you to read it; it's in your hands because you were meant to read it.

It's time.

Time to start really looking at what is going on in our lives. Not the "reality" that is in our minds or on screen, but the stripped down, honest version of what is happening in the moments, days, weeks and years that make up our lives.

So many of us are living the lives we think we are supposed to, rather than living the extraordinary life we are capable of. We settle for what society tells us we should have and what should matter to us. We miss out on not only what is possible, but much worse, we miss out on who we actually are.

We have so much passion for who was just signed to our favorite sports team, we wrap ourselves up in the juicy details of a celebrity relationship, we get engrossed in the daily political headlines, and count down to the release of the latest piece of technology. Yet, we spend almost none of that attention, emotion, or energy on ourselves.

We are given all the tools to create our own lives, yet we never pick up the hammer and start.

I hope this book helps you take a different look at your life and all the moments that make it up. To choose to truly and unapologetically live and share all of who you are with the world around you. Not just the parts you think are worthy. To finally give yourself permission to be you.

Not only do you owe it to yourself, but more importantly THE WORLD NEEDS YOU. (T.W.N.Y.)

We don't need the newer, shinier, younger, or skinnier version of you. We don't need the version you think you are supposed to be. The world needs the unfiltered version of the real you. Not how you think you should act or what you think you should do. The world needs the version of you that finds your soul on fire with energy and life. The you that feels like you are overflowing with endless possibility and the feeling that you literally don't have the time to do and be all that you are capable of. This book is about unleashing the gift that you are and the possibility of the life you could live. To stop putting so much stock in what others think and shift your view to what you care about. What you want. What makes you feel alive and who you are. It's about falling in love with the journey and truly living. You need to become an entrepreneur in the most important business there is.

The business of you.

To take the time, energy, and love to craft the most remarkable you possible. It just might not the be version of you that you thought. *Blue Goat* is about breaking from the herd and finding what makes you uniquely you. Honoring and being true to what you think, love, feel and want to do with the precious moments that make up your life. To live life not to achieve something or make someone else happy, but to realize the fullest expression of yourself.

Before we get started, there are a few things I want you to know.

This is not a list of the top ways to find happiness. It's not a fad diet or designed to save your failing relationship. It's not based on years of research of test subjects. I didn't conduct countless surveys of people and sit down with specialists to come up with a new theory. *Blue Goat* was born out of personal, honest, and in many cases tough and emotional conversations with people who are trying to figure it all out. Your best friend, aunt, co-worker, the stranger at the grocery story, and person next to you in your cycling class. It is about taking the struggles, frustrations, and issues that I was told over and over and over by so many and paying attention. *Blue Goat* is about letting go of what you think you need to be worrying about. Instead, focusing on you. Your experiences. Your opportunities. Your choices. Your life.

It begins with you.

It's time to determine if you know who you are, where you are, and where you are going. Otherwise, you may end up as just another sheep in the herd on your way to wherever everyone else thinks you should end up. Figure out where you want to go and more importantly what you want to do. In this one life make choices that fill you up and leave your stamp on the world.

It's time to become a Blue Goat.

A Blue Goat, you ask?

Yea, a Blue Goat.

What the hell is a Blue Goat?

YOU are a Blue Goat. You just don't know it yet.

In becoming a Blue Goat, you will fundamentally change the way you show up in the world and how you live your life. You will finally be giving everyone else the greatest gift there is.

The real you.

3 BLUE DOT

In the journey of becoming a Blue Goat you first must find out who and where you are.

Whenever we are lost or looking for directions in life, we reach into our pocket or purse and take out our phone. We punch in our security code, tap on our map or navigation app and hit the button that shows our exact location. When the GPS coordinates figure out where you are, a blue dot appears and places you right in the middle of the map.

A blue dot, that is you. Right now, this very second. Your place in the world at this moment in time.

When we have a place we need to get to it's easy to know what destination to put in the app. You let it use your current location as the starting point and where it puts the red pin for your destination is the bar to meet your friends for drinks after work, the airport for your trip, the park for the soccer game, the vacation spot, or your friend's house. The map drops the red pin for the destination and gives you 2-3 ways to get there. We almost always look for the quickest and fastest route. It is usually based on using the highway and getting there as quickly as possible. You pick the route and then it tells you how long it will take. That coolly programmed voiced tells you where to go, when to turn, and how to get to the red pin.

On your phone when your blue dot gets to the red pin, you have arrived at your destination. The vacation starts, the partying begins, and the family fun can finally take place. The travel is about getting somewhere to begin or start whatever is next.

That is not how the navigation system works when it comes to your life.

In the navigation that is our life, the moment that the blue dot gets to the red pin is when you will be taking your last breaths. Everything you do is part of the long journey. Getting to the red pin is the last day of your life.

So how do you choose what direction to take and what path you should use for the journey of your life? How do you determine where your blue dot should go today, tomorrow, and the next day? Where have you put your red pin on the map of your life? Have you ever changed where it is? Has your destination in life been the same place since you were a teenager, or in your 20's? Are you still heading to the same place you wanted to get to back then?

When choosing where to put your red pin, were you given guidance from everyone else, or have you decided for yourself where you want to end up? Did your parents make you give them the code to your phone, put in a destination and hand the phone back to you? Are you heading where they want you to go? Was that years ago, and you are still heading in the same direction, never realizing you can pull out your phone and change it?

Are you simply looking over at your friends' phones to see where they dropped their red pins and put yours close by? Are you worried about making sure you end up at the same place they do? If your friend decides to move where his red pin is and change where he wants to go, does that change where you want to go too?

In your one life is everyone else telling you where to go rather than you choosing where you want to end up?

When I ask people "what is your goal in life?" they often look at me confused. They've been so busy living and trying to do and be everything that they never actually stop to think about what they are trying to do and where they want to end up. Yes, they want to "be successful", have enough money to retire, or pay for college for their kids, but what do they actually want out of life?

When you choose your route, what are you focused on? Is the goal to get on the highway and speed to try and get to what's next?

How many times in life have you gotten to the "next step" in life and looked back and realized how quickly the last year has gone? How fast the last five years flew by, or even an entire decade?

Having your baby and holding him or her in your arms isn't reaching the red pin. Buying your new home isn't reaching the red pin; graduating from college isn't reaching the red pin, and getting married isn't making it to your destination. Your life is made up of countless moments and events. We think that getting to a certain milestone is the end, but the next second still happens, the clock keeps ticking, and your life keeps moving. The moments come and go, and the blue dot that is you keeps moving. Every moment in your life, whether good or bad, is simply part of the long journey to your destination and the last breaths of your life.

So how do you spend your time on the road?

Why are you trying to get to the next event, next moment, next milestone so quickly?

As soon as you get there, that moment will come and go too.

Instead of enjoying the weeks leading up to your wedding, you say, "*I'm so ready for all this prep work to be over, let's just get married already.*" The big day will arrive, the dancing will end, and the cake will be gone, and you will be married, but you can never go back and enjoy the moments and time leading up to the big day.

I can't tell you how many times people have said to me "*I would love to go back to _____ time in my life. I didn't realize how much fun it was then.*" Yet when they were there, they didn't appreciate it, didn't enjoy it, and now the time has passed.

We all go through so much of our lives, quickly wanting to get to what is next, what is next, what is next, what is next, without ever enjoying what is. We yearn for what is to come, without ever living what is here today. Leaving moment after moment unlived.

The moment right now, the gift that today is. The day you will never have again. Each day has the same amount of time, yet there are so few that we actually remember or care about.

The big presentation at work you are excited for, your child's 16th birthday, the important talk with your girlfriend's parents, the new job starting next week. All days that will be filled with important moments, but what about the countless days in between?

Can you only recall what happened on most days based on what was on TV that night, and nothing else?

You can quickly be moving along your path, getting closer and closer to the red pin without paying attention to anything else that is going on around you. Do we even consider an alternate route? We know we are going to get to the red pin eventually, but what if we spent the time along the way there differently? Should we start to pay more attention to the road we are on and where we are going?

It's possible that for July 4th weekend, everyone thinks going to the beach is a great idea. You know there will be traffic, it's going to suck and take forever, but you go anyway. You never miss the beach on the 4th.

What about the journey of your life?

If you are on the highway of your life driving in heavy traffic, does that mean everyone is trying to get to the same destination as you? "*How is it possible that we are all going to the same place? I can't believe all of the traffic!*" you think. How is it possible that in this one life you have there would be a paved highway that can take you exactly where you want to go? How does anyone other than you know where you want to go? "*There is no way this road should be here*" you start thinking.

You realize that there is only one you. With all your personal intricacies, thoughts and emotions only you can have. In your goal of making the most out of your life, there should be only one person on your journey.

I don't mean you don't have companions of all kinds: friends, lovers, family. If we are lucky, we share our lives with many others, but no one else is making the same life you are. No one else is supposed to be doing exactly what you are doing. So, you must be heading in the wrong direction. How is it possible that not only your red pin, but the route to get there is the same as everyone else's? For much of life, you will find that you are using the highway. You are with millions of other cars.

The congestion, traffic, smog, and frustration of being on the same road and heading in the same direction as everyone else can be stifling. When you were younger, you thought you were going to do and be something different and special; yet over time you somehow ended up in traffic on the highway headed in the same direction as everyone else.

You can feel the stress, anxiety, and worry building as everyone else is trying just as hard to get to and have the same things you are. There are so many people around you. The cars, the exhaust, the speed of everyone moving so frantically in the same direction can be overwhelming. Yet year after year, you drive along with the masses. Even when you need to stop and slow down, you are barely present because you are thinking about the people that are still on the highway getting ahead of you. The moments that should capture your attention are lost because you are thinking about being on the road, catching up and getting back in the race.

Checking emails during your child's play, texting while at a special dinner with friends, scrolling through Facebook while talking on the phone to your friend who needs your help, or just lost in the thoughts of what you need to do tomorrow instead of listening to your boyfriend's frustrations about his day. We are constantly consumed by the race and the highway. Not losing our spot, getting passed, and doing everything we can to make great time and get to the next thing as fast as we can. Constantly thinking about the other cars around us and making sure we are doing everything we can to keep up or pass them.

As you are driving along, it somehow dawns on you. Maybe it was an old song on the radio that made you think back to when you were a kid, or you hit a pothole that rattled you awake. You notice that you've been driving along the road, but not really paying attention. For most of the time you feel like your head is somewhere else, but suddenly you think about the directions on your phone and where you are going.

You pull out your phone again and take a close look at your red pin. You never really checked to see where your destination was set to. You look at the navigation app and squint at the screen, but can't tell where your red pin is. The map is too far out, and you can just see the blue dot and a long line to the red pin.

You spread your fingers on the screen and zoom in.

You finally see it. It's not just your red pin at the end of the journey. You can now see that there are tens of hundreds of thousands and almost an infinite number of red pins all scattered within a few feet of one another at the end of the road.

"What the hell?"

It's one thing for all of us to end up at the beach for a long weekend, but there is no way we are all supposed to end up in the same exact destination in our lives.

"This isn't right…. what am I doing? Where are we all going??"

"I gotta get the hell outta here! I'm not supposed to be on this road!!"

You think back to being younger and all that you wanted for your life. Yet here you are, living in a way that is so far removed from what you had planned for.

You realize you are speeding along on the highway of life with everyone else heading to the same place. You are doing 76mph in the 65mph HOV lane, and there are three lanes to your right packed with more cars. Each lane is almost bumper to bumper, but everyone is going at least 70mph and most cars even faster than that. You look at the cars all around you and begin to feel anxious and overwhelmed about the reality of what is happening. Just then you see the green exit sign approaching on the right. As it gets closer you can see what it says.

Next exit ½ mile.

"*I'm about to piss a lot of people off*," you think. You realize that trying to get off the highway that everyone else is on is going to be tough, but you know you have to do it.

It's time to get off the highway.

You put your blinker on and start to slow down and look over your right shoulder trying to find a break in traffic. You realize that most of the cars going by don't even see your light click on and off signaling you are trying to move over.

The first car passes and you can see the husband and wife arguing in the front seats. They aren't paying any attention to you and barely even look at the road as they speed by. In the next car is a guy wearing sunglasses and you can't tell if he is asleep at the wheel or just doesn't care as he zooms past.

*Click…clock…click…clock…click…*your turn signal keeps blinking.

You are looking back and forth at the road and over your shoulder, feeling the frustration of every extra moment heading in the wrong direction. "*Come ON people, I gotta get OVER!!*" Car after car flies by, appearing to go even faster now, and you realize that you might have to stick your neck out a bit and maybe even risk an accident to get off the highway.

You start to ease over into the lane to your right, and the car behind you slams on their horn! They continue coming, you can hear their engine rev as they move right up to the side of your car, but you hold true and keep moving over. They honk again and again, switching hands as they swing their arms in the air, disgusted at your move.

You pull all the way over and make it into the lane. As you look in the rearview mirror, you can see them angrily barking at you and then a repulsed middle finger in all of its road-rage glory on full display for your viewing pleasure.

¼ mile to next exit.

Two more lanes to go.

You feel like Frogger trying to not get squashed scrambling between the traffic, but know you need to get to the exit and off the highway. More cars roaring by. More people focused so much on speeding along and getting to what is next, indifferent to anyone else on the road. A fleet of eighteen wheelers is approaching, and you know you have to act fast. Your tires screech as you swerve over in front of the first truck in a small space between it and a minivan that just passed. You can feel the weight and power of it barreling down on you as the loud horn wraps your car in a fuming blast of frustration. You turn to see the grill coming within what seems like inches of your car out of the back window.

HOOOOOOOOONNNNNNNNNKKKKKKKK! HOONKKK! HOOOOOOOOOONNNNKK!!

The horn of the eighteen-wheeler blasts again and again. Undeterred, you look over your shoulder through the side window to your right again.

One more lane to go.

An older couple is now next to you. They are going the speed limit and not fast enough to pass you, but too slow at the same time. You feel stuck. You aren't going to make it. You try slowing down, but there is nowhere to go, the car behind them is too close, and you are out of options.

Exit 1000 feet.

You make the move. You are almost side by side with the older couple, but turn into them anyway. As you come within inches of crashing into the side of their car, they quickly swerve to the right to avoid you side-swiping them and head down the exit ramp with you.

Racing down the off-ramp, you are side by side. The wife is laying on the horn, and the husband in the passenger seat is frantically waving his arms. You can see how flustered and scared his wife is behind the wheel. You slow down and let them pull ahead of you as you head down the off-ramp. As they reach the stop sign, you can see the lights change as they shift the car into park. They both get out of the car and slam their doors. They come storming over to your window.

"*What the hell is wrong with you! Are you freaking crazy?!?! Did you not see us!! You almost got us killed!*" they yell. "*I know, I'm so sorry, but I had to get off!*" you reply.

As they continue to berate you with a torrent of obscenities, you look over them, and you realize something. You were hoping they could just drive back onto the highway, but there is no onramp. Noticing where you are looking, the wife turns and notices, saying, "*Now we can't even get back on the highway. Thanks a lot!*" "*What do we do now?*" the husband adds.

The husband pulls out his phone to try and find another way to get back on the highway as you continue to apologize profusely to his wife for almost causing an accident and messing up their trip. Just then the husband taps the wife on the shoulder. "*Hey, didn't you always want to go to the mountain falls? It looks like they are just a little while down this road. I never knew that this is where they were. We weren't planning on it, but maybe we should go since we are so close by.*" They turn and talk between themselves for a few seconds and then tell you to be more careful of others and to not drive like such a lunatic.

They half thank you and smile as they head back to their car and drive off to see the cascading waterfall they had always talked about seeing, but didn't know was here because they were too busy racing along the highway to notice.

You turn right and end up behind the couple again and drive behind them for a mile or so, being sure to give them enough space so they don't think you are following them. You come to a T in the road and watch as they slowly turn left, heading towards the mountain falls. With no cars coming from either direction and an empty road behind, you pull out your phone and hit the GPS button to see where your blue dot is.

Now that you are off the highway you notice something. Before, when you looked at the map, you only saw the highway and the line taking your blue dot directly to the red pin. Now you have to use your fingers to zoom in on the map. There are so many more roads to choose from. You went from being on one road with everyone else to almost countless possibilities of different ways you could go. Thousands of roads, and even open fields that can take you just about anywhere you want.

After thinking more about your experience on the highway, you realize that you don't want to end up where everyone else does. The journey isn't going to be any fun, and you are going to be constantly dealing with everyone else. You realize that while you were on the highway, the middle finger, the stress, other people's anger and all their frustrations started to affect you. Emotionally you felt all the crap from those around you changing who you were. You also realize you had no idea why you were heading towards the red pin. Somewhere along the journey you simply found yourself on the highway with everyone else, never really looking to see if you knew where you were headed.

Now, on a side road, you realize that there are almost no cars around. For the first time, you see how much the view has changed. Instead of keeping the windows up to block the noise and exhaust fumes you can roll them down. The clean, fresh breeze hits your face. You take in a deep breath. You can see more of the country-side. The scenery shifts from cars and concrete to a dirt road, trees and the sun relaxing in the afternoon sky. You can almost feel your energy level changing. The franticness of it all. Trying to keep up with all the people and everyone around you. The sheer weight of the masses all trying to get to the same place.

You don't have to deal with it anymore.

You ease over onto the shoulder, the tires first finding the loose gravel, then the edge of the grass. You slowly come to a stop and shift the car into park. You look through the front windshield at the world around you.

You look back down at your phone again. You see the blue dot. You know exactly where it is. You click in the directions and want to change where to put the red pin. Only now you are struck by a new worry.

You feel lost.

It's scary, because you don't know where you are going.

There was a certain comfort in being with everyone else, because at least on the highway you weren't alone. Yea, it was hectic and busy, but there was also a certain level of comfort in the sheer fact that you were with everyone else.

Now it's just you. If you take a wrong turn, if you end up in the wrong place, you have no one to blame but yourself. Your stress level starts to rise and all of a sudden you have a burning desire to get back on the highway. You were on it for so long. It's all you've ever known. Not much time has passed, but part of you already misses the pace, the stress, and the craziness of everyone.

You liked looking at the other cars going by. You didn't realize it, but you were curious to see what type of car everyone was driving, and it was fun watching the people argue with one another. The entertainment of the person singing and dancing to the music, or the test of trying to out-maneuver another car through the traffic and make better time.

Now it's just you. You realize that you aren't going to be able to spend all your time frustrated with how the others are driving and whether people are going too fast or too slow. You can't complain about the traffic, the tailgaters, the noise, and the exhaust fumes.

It's all gone now. All that's left is you.

What's next?

For the first time, you realize that you have all the control. You get to decide what the next turn or direction will be.

Maybe I'll just keep driving for a while and see what I find. I'm sure I'll come across something that I'll want to check out, or maybe a fun place to eat. What road do I want to turn down next? Do I simply want to keep driving along the creek that is on the side of the road and see where it takes me? You have one hundred percent control of what your next step in life is. No one else is telling you where you need to be headed, and you aren't stuck going in the same direction as everyone else. On your phone, the blue dot isn't moving but slowly expanding and contracting. Almost like a small blue dot that is breathing.

That's you.

You look back out to the road and even consider pulling off and driving through the fields. There are no fences. You could blaze an entirely new trail and go off-roading if you wanted.

It hits you; you finally realize what has been going on.

In your life, you've always been so worried about keeping up and not falling behind. You've always looked at the map and felt so limited. The directions were simple. Get in line and head down the road with everyone else. Now, for the first time, you realize something entirely different. You are in complete control of not only where you are, but where each decision is going to take you.

It's almost overwhelming now. The possibilities. Before, you almost felt stuck in your life. Yea, you could move between the lanes, but you were headed in just one direction. Now that you are off the highway and paying attention, you realize just how unlimited your options are. You can do and be anything you could ever want. It took you getting off the highway of life where you needed to "stay in your lane" to the boundless potential that your life gives you each day.

In your head, you can hear the voice: "*We always talk about off-roading, but never ever do it! Let's give it a go!! Let's do this!!!*"

"*I hear you*"...you think as you smile. It's time.

About fifty feet up you see an opportunity and pull off the road and turn into the field. At first, you aren't sure if you should be doing it or not. You take a deep breath, not knowing what's ahead. You slowly start to inch the car over the grass, rocks and dirt; you can sense the car getting used to being off the perfectly paved highway.

You feel the tall grass begin to hit the underside of your car. As you start to slowly go faster, it begins making an almost rhythmic pitter patter on the front bumper. You realize there is no road to follow. You press down on the gas and start to go faster and faster as the grass and weeds make louder music. You make slight turns to your left and right, feeling the car swing and fishtail in the field. You swerve around a small tree, hitting the last few branches with the back of your car, sending leaves into the sky.

You speed up and can feel a smile start to creep across your face as you push the accelerator down even further. Forty-one mph...47mph...56mph...the music on the bumper gets louder. You drive over bushes as the car hops and bounds over small holes in the ground as you speed over the open field. You swing your arms across your body and lean over as you slam on the brakes and turn the wheel hard to the right. Everything goes into slow motion, and you can feel the tires slide over the top of the tall grass to your left as you perform a wide skid across the earth.

The car rocks back and forth and comes to a stop. With both hands on the wheel, you look out over the dashboard. All you see is the open field. Your smile broadens. You can feel the warm sensation of pure energy building in your stomach. It's getting louder and brighter, and you feel small needles and goosebumps on your arms and all the way up through your head. Even though you are in the car, it feels like the heat of the hot summer sun has just come from behind a building and is engulfing the car and you. You notice the birds chirping. "*I haven't heard a bird in years,*" you think. You can hear the crickets talking to one another. You hear the grass and trees swaying in the wind.

You can feel your life.

Everything that you hadn't noticed for years is now registering, and you can see and sense so much around you. You went from looking at the world through an old cable TV to experiencing everything in IMAX ultra-high definition. You look down at your arms and notice for the first time all the small freckles, small moles, and the millions of individual hairs. You turn your hands over and notice every crease, every line, every detail. I never noticed any of this stuff before, you think. You realize the beauty of every small thing going on in the world around you and even the amazing parts of yourself that you never took time to explore or pay attention to.

You look back at your phone. The way you look at your navigation app changes completely. You can feel your heart beating and have finally found out exactly where you are. You have found your blue dot. For the first time, you realize that you don't need to care about where the red pin is.

It doesn't matter.

The only thing that matters is where you decide the blue dot is going next. From here your life is a limitless field of possibilities. Do you keep driving across the grass, do you head left and go up the hill, or do you just sit here and relax for a while?

All that matters is that the blue dot is exactly where it is supposed to be. Right now, this very moment, how you choose to spend your time. Where you want to be. What you know honors how valuable and important each moment of your life is. If you keep moving the blue dot to where exactly on the map it is supposed to be, then whenever that red pin drops and you take your last breath, you will be exactly where you are supposed to be.

We never know when the red pin is going to drop on the map saying that the journey is over. We can't plug the destination of life in our GPS. We can't look and see how many miles, minutes, or years it will be until we get there. We don't know. So being concerned about that unknown future is a waste of our time and energy. You can spend all your time worrying about when the red pin will drop, but that won't change it.

Instead, we need to change the way we look at our journey.

If all you focus is on your blue dot, you will be present for every moment and will make sure that you are always exactly where you want to be in life. You will not look up and realize when your last day comes that it's too late to change who and where you are and wish your blue dot could be somewhere else entirely. Where your blue dot is right now is important, but what matters so much more is where it will be in an hour, later today, tomorrow, next week and a month from now.

When we are lost, and looking for another route, your map will typically say *Recalculating…*

Sometimes that is the greatest gift you can give yourself. A chance at choosing a new path, a new direction and starting a new journey.

First, you must figure out where you are today. You have to look inside. To examine every aspect of your life to see if you are who and where you want to be. Once you figure that out, then you finally know where your blue dot is. The next step will chart the course for the life you will live. Heading closer to the red pin with everyone else, or living your life.

You are not one to just follow the other cars. It's time to get the hell off the highway and head down the exit. You aren't about being and doing what others have done before. Your life isn't about following anyone else.

When you come to the T in the road, it isn't about taking the road less traveled. In your one shot at this life it is about finding the courage to do so much more. It is about staring into the wilderness and blazing a new trail.

Becoming a Blue Goat is about creating a new road that no one has ever been down before.

Your road.

4 THE HERD

On the Nature Channel, every week they have countless shows highlighting animals from all over the world. Shows about every shape and size, and how all of them live. One of the most common animals, with a current population of over one billion, is the sheep.

Sheep are domesticated and raised so they can be used for their wool, milk, and meat. A group or gathering of sheep is called a herd. The interesting thing about domesticated sheep is that their wool can have a wide range of colors from pure white all the way to dark brown or black. Some sheep are even known to have spotted wool.

The primary use is to take their wool for commercial production and profit. Even though the sheep look so different from one another, they are raised and live for the benefit of others. While one sheep might have white fur and another may have dark fur, at the end of the day they are all sheep.

They are considered flock animals; and have a natural tendency to live in a dominance hierarchy where they follow a leader. Sheep tend to want to keep together in herding patterns and typically show stress when separated from the rest of the flock members.

In many cases, they won't just follow the older sheep, but will follow the one that is the first to move. So, while there do appear to be leaders of the herd, if one sheep starts off in a different direction, it can acquire a following simply because that sheep was the first to do something new. Not wanting to be left behind, the rest of the sheep and the herd will stop grazing and follow the new leader.

One farmer may be able to easily herd countless sheep due to the flocking behavior and desire of the sheep to stay together. It has even been shown that their position in the moving flock is highly correlated to some sort of social structure. Sheep are not considered highly intelligent. They are placed just below pigs on the IQ scale.

They are typically known for their sounds, the well-known "baaing" noise that they make. Sheep also make what are called "bleats," which are more distinctive individual sounds that allows them to communicate with one another.

So...sheep are herd animals with cognitive abilities, whose actions are often determined by a social hierarchy. While they may appear different based on the color of their fur they are very much the same underneath.

Most notably, while they may be following the herd and dealing with social dynamics, they don't know it, but they were bred, fed and live to make other people money from their milk, meat, and wool.

So why does this matter? When looking at it abstractly can we take what we see about sheep and compare it to our lives and the way our society works? Are there similarities? Do we even want to admit the possibility that it is so much more?

Are we all just sheep?

Are we living a life where we follow the more dominant leaders, or get caught up in and quickly follow someone who is a trendsetter or simply the first to do something? Do we follow because of what they do and where they are going, or just that they were the first to do it? Are we more concerned about being left behind and not being part of the herd and keeping up with everyone else or do we actually know where the herd is going?

When one sheep takes off in a certain direction, do we blindly follow, or do we know why they are doing what they are doing? Do we ask why they do certain things, or not concern ourselves with that? Are we afraid and worried about being left behind? Does it feel more secure to be right in the middle, trying not to stand out, knowing that so many others are in the same position, or are we okay to make decisions on our own?

Does being in the herd, but just on the edge or near the front make us feel like we are doing something different or special? Even though at the end of the day we are still going to go along with everyone else? If the herd begins to leave us behind, do we feel stressed or worried about being on our own? If we fall behind, is our sole focus and all our energy spent trying to get caught back up?

Have we ever taken the time to stick our heads up to look and see where we are and where we are going, or are we too consumed with comparing ourselves to all the sheep around us? Like the cars on the highway, do we just assume that since we are all headed in the same direction it must be a good place to go to?

Do we spend all our time bleating with one another and worrying about who is going where rather than asking bigger questions like why are we in this fenced-in area and where are they taking us?

Within the herd do we find ourselves seeking out those other sheep that have wool that looks like ours, and do we let the one with the spotted wool or different color wool in our area? Do we try to make real connections with the other sheep, or do we simply want to know what part of the field they grew up on, what part of the farm they live in, and whether they are in front of us or behind us in the herd?

Who are the sheep that are the leaders of the everyone?

Do we take the time to find out who they are and why they are leading, or are they simply in charge because they have been around the longest or because they intimidate the other sheep? Were they just the first to do something and now other sheep are following them, or do they know where they are going?

Are the leaders of the sheep trying to take care of the entire herd and do what is best for everyone, or are they simply trying to stay in front so they can be the first to feed or have the best views?

Who is the farmer in all of this?

Is the farmer taking care of the sheep because he truly loves them and wants what is best for the sheep, or does he have other motives? Are they there for the sheep, or are the sheep there to benefit the farmer? Why does the farmer spend so much time, energy and effort to take care of the sheep and raise them? Is the herd being taken care of to use the strength of the sheep, their milk, wool and meat? Do we give up everything of who we are, how we spend our time, where we give our money and at the end potentially our lives to serve someone else's purpose?

Does the farmer have parallels to our society? Are the businesses and companies that tell us everything we need and want to hear about ourselves doing those things to help us or to get us to buy something? Are we being led to where we need to go, or to the place that will benefit someone else?

At the end of the day, are we all sheep that are here to provide something for others? Our work, our energy, our time, our money, are all those things for someone else's benefit, and we just don't see it? Do we see that at a certain level we may be exploited and herded in a way that isn't to our benefit? Would the farmer spend all that time, effort and energy on just one sheep? Would they spend the same amount of money on feed, land, housing, and care for the wool, milk and meat of just one of sheep? Would companies spend millions of dollars advertising, marketing, promoting and selling their product to just one of us? Or, do they need countless sheep to provide them with what they need? Is the success of the farmer based on just a few of the sheep following along? Or does the farmer need the entire herd to follow?

Where are you in all of this?

Are you simply another sheep following the herd?

What is the other option? Do we even have one?

Some sheep see what is going on. They realize that they are in the big herd. They may try and quickly start running in a certain direction and find out, much to their amazement, they are being followed by other sheep. They enjoy the influence and excitement that comes from realizing that the other sheep will follow them. They have a following of other sheep simply because they were the first to do something, but in the bigger picture, they are all still moving along with the rest of the sheep in the larger herd.

Some realize that they are sheep and their goal is to simply stand out from the crowd. We all know the black sheep. They might try to stand out from the others or do things solely to draw attention to themselves or try and be different. At the end of the day, they are still just another sheep in the herd.

When moving outside the fences, do the sheep realize there are no actual barriers or boundaries to them leaving? Even without fences, do we allow the boundaries that we create in our minds to dictate the actions that we take in our lives? Are the sheep so consumed with looking at each other and seeing who is doing what that they don't even realize when they aren't within the fence?

When moving together outside of the fence do we allow stress and worry to keep us with the herd? Do we feel like we can't go on our own, assume we can't leave, or fear missing out on what is happening with everyone else?

Is there the possibility for so much more?

You can only determine your direction in life by first finding your current location. You are the blue dot. The deeper question is whether or not you are a sheep. You may be a leader, or right in the middle of the pack but either way you may be another sheep in the massive herd.

So, what else can we be? Who can you be?

A goat.

A goat is a close relative to the sheep and is also domesticated. Females are "does," and males are "bucks or billies," The juveniles are called kids.

Goats are naturally curious. They are known to love exploring their surroundings and the world around them. They don't allow their surroundings to dictate their lives; even though they have hooves, they have been found climbing trees.

They are extremely inquisitive about the world around them, which makes them very difficult to herd and keep in pens or fenced areas. It has been shown that keeping a goat in an enclosure is difficult because they are constantly looking and testing for ways to get out. Goats can be extremely creative in finding ways to escape. When put into a pen, goats quickly realize that they are being confined. They seem to have an innate desire to break free and escape from captivity.

Upon escaping, they are okay being around other goats, but they desire the ability to search, explore and seek out new experiences and new things rather than being in a pen.

So how do we determine if we are a sheep or a goat?

Do we think we are a goat, yet are simply a sheep that is standing on the side of the herd? Are we one of the sheep that think we are a goat, because we are the first to do something and others follow?

Are we in charge of other sheep or in an important role, but have forgotten that we are really doing the same thing as other sheep in jobs just like us? Maybe we just happen to be older sheep or have a fancy job title.

Or are we an actual goat that looks at the enclosure, the fence, and the fact that the farmer isn't there to take care of us but wants something from us? Do we focus our attention on getting out of the herd and exploring the world around us to see what we may find, or are we afraid of what is on the other side of the fence? Do we worry more about what the other sheep will think of us, rather than what we may find if we do something different?

Do we even know where the herd is right now? Do we have a picture of exactly where our blue dot is on the map in this huge group? Or are we simply going along with all the other sheep with no attention being paid to what is happening, more worried about being left behind or trying to keep up?

In our lives, have we ever taken the time to figure out where it is that we want to go?

Are we exploring the world around us like a goat and tasting things and climbing trees, or are we stuck with whatever we are being fed by the farmer?

Can we do something different?

There is a chance.

The herd comes to a small rise and there are a few rocks, and you step up and are able for the first time to look back over the entire herd. Tens of thousands and millions of sheep. More than you can see; you had no idea there were so many. Miles and miles and miles of sheep. Everyone following along and walking together. There are more than you can count. Over the horizon, you can barely make them out one by one because there are so many. As you look back, you can see movement in different directions. Like birds in the wind, you see small groups moving around, but they are all within the herd heading in the same direction.

Like smog hanging over the city, the air is thick with dust and the strong odor from the herd.

You can see how muddy the masses are from all walking along the same path and tearing up the earth below. There is slop being given in different buckets, and you can hear the constant drone and noise of all the bleating between the sheep.

It is then you look over and see. On a field, a few hundred yards away, something is moving that catches your eye. You watch as it runs and zigzags through the fields and then bounds up a hillside, climbs over a pile of rocks and back down. It is exploring everything around it. As it walks, there is a lightness about it, and you can almost feel the energy and bounce in each step. It almost appears to be hopping. Some dark animal that you can't quite figure out what it is.

It is looking around, and you can see it raise its head to feel the wind and the full power of the sun on its face. It is eating fresh cut grass that hasn't been trampled on by all the other sheep. It isn't eating up the slop that the farmer is giving out.

You turn and see all the sheep behind you. Heads down. Tails down. All walking in unison. Like old elephants dragging each foot step by slow step, the herd moves with what seems to be a heavy weight. The sheer size of the group is overwhelming.

The clouds above begin to move, and you catch a bit of the cool breeze from the field close by. You can smell the pollen from the flowers and hints of fresh grass in the air. Walking slower now, the animal is getting closer. It appears from behind the trunk of a large tree.

A goat.

As the clouds part and the sunlight peeks through, the light hits the goat, and it stops. As it slowly turns its head towards the breeze, you can finally see it. Its fur is a vibrant, radiant blue. Like the color of the beautiful blue of the open ocean, it has a shininess to it that comes alive in the sunlight.

A Blue Goat.

You watch as it's ears twist and turn to pick up every sound as it continues to look around. It is paying attention to everything. The Blue Goat surveys the land and bounds off to a nearby tree. Even though it has hoofs, it scales the bark of the tree and finds a spot on one of the branches. It sits on its hind legs and folds its front legs across the branch.

The Blue Goat looks up and watches the branches and leaves slowly shifting and moving in the afternoon wind. It lowers its gaze to survey the brush and appears to be watching a small animal. You can see its head trace the movement of something. The animal in the brush is moving all over, and you can see its senses heighten watching and tracing each movement below. The Blue Goat glances to the right, and you can sense that it is examining the land and trying to figure out where to go next.

Its breath is calm and appears to have a slow and deliberate motion to it. As it inhales and exhales, you see the Blue Goat's diaphragm slowly moving like the pulsing blue GPS dot on your phone.

It knows right where it is.

The Blue Goat turns from scanning the distant horizon and looks your way. As an older sheep, you look back and then without realizing what is happening, you lock eyes. You sense the Blue Goat's remarkable energy. You can feel the power of its presence and confidence. Its eyes have the darkest black center. Around the pupils, you see yellow flecks and a greenish blue background that make the eyes look like bright sunflowers in an open field.

You can feel it.

Something about that look makes you think back. You start to replay your life. You feel the movie being shown.

You can finally see it all.

You remember being a young sheep and your friends making fun of you for how curly your wool was. You remember thinking how much it upset you, worrying that they weren't going to like you and something was wrong because your wool was so different. You remember all the time you spent stressing over trying to change it to make it look like all your friends. Now all your wool had been shorn off and was gone.

You think about all the time you spent worrying about what your friends thought about you. You were so concerned about being left behind that you constantly felt exhausted and stressed out. You were worried about making your parents proud and trying to be noticed and stand out in the huge herd.

You remember how it felt when you started to get a bit older. You had the best section of the fenced-in area for your family and all your friends were jealous of your view and the new wood they just installed in your pen. Even then, you still didn't know where you were going. Your children were following you now. You wanted to set the example and lead, but you still just trotted after those sheep that appeared to have it all together.

It seems like so long ago and yet it feels like just yesterday you were a young sheep.

The Blue Goat continues to look directly at you, then slowly releases your stare.

It looks behind you, and you can see its head gently move as it continues to trace the outline of the entire heard for miles and miles behind you. It lifts its head up as it tries to see the end of the herd over the horizon. It sits up and then stands to try and get a better view of how far back it goes. You watch as the Blue Goat extends its neck and gets on the top of its hooves to try and see just how many sheep there are.

Perched up on the branch, the Blue Goat watches them all moving together. It hears all the bleating and baaing which makes it almost impossible to hear any one sheep over any other.

You turn and look also.

Like all the cars stuck on the highway together going to the same place, you can see all the sheep jammed together, moving in unison to some unknown destination. You can see the dust; you notice how lifeless so many of them appear to be. So many of the sheep look sick and unhappy. They are all constantly getting in each other's way and snipping at one another. They continue to move around, jockeying for position.

The Blue Goat's eyes retrace the outline of the herd all the way back to you. You look down to see your old hairless body and the dirt and grime of a life lived within the herd.

It looks towards the tree and shakes its body like a dog getting rid of water after a bath. With a quick surveying look to the ground, it jumps towards the trunk of the tree and with a pounce off the bark lands effortlessly on the ground.

You watch as the Blue Goat takes a few steps ahead. It picks a spot and rolls over onto the ground, twisting and turning on its back all over the bright green grass. As it leans to one side, it smells the white and yellow flowers around it. It takes a bite of a tall shrub and chews on the long leaves. The long stalks stick out of both sides of its mouth. It looks like a dog with a large bone. After a few more twists and rolls, it leans over onto its side and stands up on all four legs.

It looks over to you again.

With a parting half smile, you can feel the look. It reminds you of the one your parents gave you when you didn't make the team, or your girlfriend broke up with you. "*Sorry it didn't work out the way you wanted.*" The Blue Goat has a solemn face as it shrugs its shoulders towards you.

The clouds shift in the sky above, and you can see the Blue Goat look ahead out at the horizon. The Blue Goat takes a few cautious steps, trying to determine exactly which way it wants to go. It pauses with its front left leg in the air, curiously scanning to its left and right.

Its tail flickers and you can see the Blue Goat's senses taking in everything going on around it. Looking, deciding, thinking and pondering what to do next.

Like the driver realizing it can get off the highway, the Blue Goat sees that the options are endless. It can go anywhere it wants and do anything it wants. It isn't held back by the weight of the herd; it doesn't care what the other sheep are doing, or where they are going.

The Blue Goat knows that it is only responsible for finding its own path and journey.

And then, in an instant, it was off. Bounding ahead. Darting back and forth across the grass and over bushes. Excitedly spinning in a complete 360 sometimes as it ran; looking around and surveying the exact path and what steps it was going to take as it went. You could feel the lightness in the journey. Unlike all the sheep where you could see and sense the regret, frustration and worry in their steps. All you could see was exhilaration, curiosity, freedom and an amazing presence about its movements. The Blue Goat was carefree and yet at the same time very deliberate. As quickly as it moved and darted back and forth, you could see that it was listening, looking and keenly aware of everything going on around it.

The Blue Goat was getting further away now. Every so often it would stop. Looking around, you could see its blue stomach slowly moving. You could tell exactly where it was from the rhythmic movement of what now looked like a blue dot on the horizon.

It observed the land ahead, but most amazingly it never looked back. Only searching for where it could go next, not where it had come from and what was part of its past. The Blue Goat either caught the scent of something it wanted to explore or found a new path, you couldn't really tell. All you could see was it disappear over the hill and off to the horizon.

It was gone.

Blue Goats are different. They aren't worried about the herd. They don't waste energy on seeing where the other sheep are in the journey. They don't care what slop the farmer is feeding them or where everyone else is going. Blue Goats aren't chasing after other sheep simply because they are the first to do something. They are listening to the world around them and paying attention to their inner guide for where they should go and what they are drawn to explore. They are much more interested in where they are going than where they've been. They know exactly where they are at each moment and because of that can quickly change direction if needed, knowing that it will lead to the next adventure, opportunity or new tree to climb. The memories of the past don't cloud the decisions and judgments of what is happening today.

The sheep are left behind. The Blue Goat is so far on its own journey that it can't even hear the bleating anymore. Long gone are the masses of sheep and the slow, lifeless movement of the herd.

The Blue Goat realized that by taking its own path, it can explore and do whatever it wants, whenever it wants. It isn't worried about whether anyone else is following because it doesn't look back to see. It doesn't care. It is more focused on what is ahead and the journey to come. It realized that in the only life it has it can never be the greatest version of itself if it is stuck with the masses. It will be confined, limited, and put in a pen; rather than be free to be itself, choose its own direction and get the absolute most out of its life.

Meeting after meeting I've had the conversations and dealt with the frustrations. The impact of a life lived in the herd.

"*Court, neither of us are happy and it is really starting to affect our marriage*", "*Life is just so exhausting that I don't know how everyone else does it*", "*All my friends have it together, they have no idea I feel this lost*", "*I just feel stuck*", "*I'm so overwhelmed with everything going on I literally don't know what I'm supposed to do*".

It's time to figure out who we are, where we are and what choices and decisions led us to get on the highway. It's time to look around and see if we are truly living our own life, or if we are just another sheep trudging along with the rest of the herd. It's time to look deeper, ask the questions and first figure out how we got to where we are.

To look at the moments, choices, and issues that lead so many to get stuck in the herd.

Only then can you become a Blue Goat.

5 BUT WHY?

We all lost that feeling somewhere along our journey. We had it when we were younger and needed the answers so badly. We were told so many different things. Sometimes we were just told, "*Because I said so.*"

Yet in life we no longer ask "why?"

As a child, you needed to know the answer. You would pester your parents and older siblings, but you had to know: "*Why do cat's meow?*" "*Why do I have a belly button?*" "*Why can't I eat ice-cream for breakfast?*"

The questions were real and the curiosity unmistakable. You weren't asking to be a pain; you were asking because there were things happening around you that you needed to understand. You had this itch that you had to scratch. You were curious about why things were the way they were; it mattered, and without the truth, you could become frustrated or even angry.

Then it changed.

We were curious about "why" so many things in our life worked the way they did, but then stopped. We gave up asking the most important question just before the answers started to matter.

"Why?"

We gave into what we were being told, fed, given, and what was expected of us.

The truth could have been so much more meaningful, unlocked new doors, kept us from making certain decisions, but we didn't get all the information we needed.

Maybe we did it out of fear. Maybe because we heard "*because that's the way it is*", "*because I'm your parent*", "*because I said so*", or "*because that is what you are supposed to do*" so many times we stopped asking.

Is that the answer to so many questions that we have in life, "*because that's the way it is*"?

What if we could get that back? What if we could start to ask not only the world around us, but ourselves "Why?" Would we finally get real answers to the questions that matter now more than ever? Could we learn what other people's motives are for wanting us to do certain things? Is it possible we would uncover what our family's expectations of us really are? For the first time, would we understand what frustrations or disappointment our spouse has? Do we realize that our friends may want us to do things to make them feel better about themselves? Would we find that most people don't know why they make the decisions they make? Why are we making the choices we are making?

Do we ask ourselves, or the people around us the real question?

"I just bought this bag the other day; you have got to go buy it!"

"You two have been together a year now; you should get married."

"I'm really not going to be successful until I make at least six figures."

"Is your car paid off? It's time for you to get a new one!"

"Those aren't in style any-more; you can't wear those!"

"I need to lose at least another 5lbs before I can do that."

Do we just accept statements like these? Do we ever ask "why" when life hands us these moments?

Here is how some of those conversations go when we ask ourselves or others "Why?"

"You are due in five months; it's time for you to start looking for a house!"

"Mom, why do I need a bigger house, when we have plenty of space in the townhome?"

"Because you are about to have a baby!"

"Yea, but we have plenty of space, we even have a guestroom we don't use, and we can put the crib in there."

"Yea, but you have a family now; you need a bigger house."

"Why?"

"Because you have a child now, you should be in a house."

"What does having a child have to do with us moving?"

"Because people with kids should raise their children in a home."

"Um, what? That doesn't make any sense. We have plenty of space and are already in a good school district."

"Well, weren't you raised in a house?!? I think you turned out pretty good, didn't you?"

"Mom, what are you talking about? We don't need to move just because we are having a baby, and we don't need to start paying more for a mortgage we don't need just because I'm going to be a mom."

"Whatever!! It's your life!"

How often do people want us to do things just because that is what they did? Us following their actions makes them feel better about who they are and what they have done and the decisions they've made in their own lives.

Us making the same choices, following the same path, deciding to live in a similar way gives them comfort. It makes others feel like they've made the right decisions and are leading for others to follow. They like looking back and seeing people in the herd behind them.

When you choose a different path, or ask them why they did something, all too often they don't even know why. They may even find it hard to answer why they did so many things or made certain decisions in their lives.

"All of my friends were doing the same thing."

"Because that is what we were told to do."

"I just assumed I was supposed to."

"We didn't know any better back then."

When we ask the question sometimes we are amazed by the real answers we find.

We learn what people project on us, their expectations, fears, and other head trash about what society thinks we are supposed to do.

What truths would we find out if we asked others or ourselves these questions? How often does someone want you to do something simply because they did it themselves? They joined a sorority, went to a certain vacation spot, used a certain tutor for their kids, so they tell you to do the same things.

Are we being told to do things, or about things because the people around you know what you need or who you are? Do you simply take whatever you are being shown, told, or given, or do you ask, "*But why do I need this?*", "*Why should I do that?*", "*Why will that make my life better?*"

When you ask "why?" the answers may startle you at first.

"Because everyone else is doing it."

"Uh, I don't know; it's just what you do."

"Because I'm your boss."

"Because that's what all of the successful guys at the firm have."

Most people don't know why they do the things they do.

In many cases, they do things because they assume they are supposed to. They think their actions are the norm and that they are fulfilling some unwritten expectations of life that they are looking to achieve or check off the list. As a result, many of us are worried about not doing certain things that everyone else is doing so we don't even ask.

Fear of not fitting in so we talk about and try to like the same thing everyone in the group does. Concern about standing out so we dress the same and shop in the same stores. Anxiety of being left behind, so we work like crazy to make more money. Fear of not being "the perfect mom" so you try to do and be involved in everything. Worry about people thinking you are successful so you get a newer car. Stress about making your parents proud so you study what you know they want you to.

Yet, we never ask the most important question which is "why"?

Why are we doing these things? Who are we doing them for?

Are the choices we are making on a daily basis because we look around to get guidance from others as to how we are supposed to live our lives? Do we know that they have put any real thought into the decisions they are making? Are they just following someone else without asking "why" themselves?

Find out what matters to the only person that matters, you.

What makes you tick, where are your values, what is going on around you that you care about, or more importantly what isn't worthy of your time?

We can learn a lot about the world if we ask better questions.

It's time to look for more.

Ask "why?". It's time to find what's real in life. You can choose not to take things at face value. You can keep from allowing others' projections on you to dictate what you do and how you live. You are strong enough and smart enough to know when life is feeding you crap, when you are being told what you want to hear, or when other people don't know what the hell they are talking about. Choose your path rather than what everyone else is doing.

A Blue Goat asks. "*Am I just going along with everyone else?*"

"Why?"

6 TOMORROW

Your co-worker, your parent or your friend asks you how things are going.

"Yea, there is stuff that isn't 'ideal,' but nobody has it all."

"I had a terrible start to the day. I can't wait until this day is over!"

"I can't just 'be happy' all of the time. That's not how life works."

"When x, y, z happens then I will be in a good place, and I'll be living the dream!"

How many times have you thought about an event, an issue, a relationship, a time in your life, or even a day as something that you are just trying to "get through"?

You were late to class and got yelled at by the teacher, totally screwed up your big presentation at the office, spilled coffee all over your work clothes and your car when slamming on the brakes during your drive to work, or got into a big fight with your girlfriend over the phone.

How many days have you said "*I just can't wait until today is over!*".

Is it possible to look at your watch and say, "*Well, this morning totally sucked, I look like crap and ran into my crush, my event was a disaster, but I have seven more hours in the day, and I only have one shot at April 23rd, 2018, and I'm not going to let a terrible morning ruin the rest of it*"?

Or, do you constantly try to get through the days just hoping that at some point you will have one that is actually good from beginning to end? Until then, do you give up at the first sign that things aren't going great?

"*Just another day I gotta get through,*" you tell yourself. "*The weekend is almost here.*"

Do the days of your life get the value they deserve? If you were told you only had eleven more days to live would you look at the days and moments differently?

Would you say, "*Yea I've got coffee all over myself, but I'm not going to be pissed all day because I literally only have ten more days left.*"

When do we get to the point where we finally decide to find value in each day? To see the gift of the moments we have and find the ability to adjust the lens through which we see the time we have left?

If you look out your window and there is a storm, you see dark clouds, heavy rain, and fierce lightning. We almost always get stuck in the storms in life. The storm is the coffee spilled on your lap or the bad presentation. The ex who won't leave you alone and calls and texts all day long, the bad news, or maybe even just a crappy meal.

We forget that it's all about how we see ourselves and with what perspective we choose to look at those moments.

If you have ever been on a plane and taken off when it is raining, you will remember flying through the thunder-clouds and breaking out of the darkness into the blue sky just above the storm. The sun greets you, and you begin to experience a totally different day. You can still see the darkness, see the lightning and can still hear the thunder that is going on at the same time, but your view has changed.

You see everything differently.

In life, you can allow yourself to be stuck in the dark cloud. You can be short with your friends, rude to your girlfriend, or even not take your dog on a walk since you are in such a bad mood, or you can say, "*Yea, it's pouring on me, but just above the rain is a bright blue sky. Just above that dark cloud, the sun is shining. It's there. I just need to think about the amazing day that is going on right now too.*"

We can allow ourselves to get caught in the storms of life, or see the much bigger picture and the beautiful day that is happening at the same time. Every day our gift of perspective will shape how we see the world and how it affects us. Just trying to get the imperfect days over with will leave you with more days missed than lived.

What would change if you were running out of days? Would the things affect you the way they do now? Would you still get as frustrated, upset, or angry?

Or, would you laugh and say, "*Screw it! I'm not going to waste my time on my ex and worry about what just happened. I can't just get through the day because I only have so many left. I'm going to think of the beautiful day that is literally going on right now just above my head.*

I'm not going to waste these moments just because they aren't what I had hoped for."

Your life is too important to let a single day be wasted.

The moments you can and should have are too precious. All too often we wait until we get older or have a health change to finally see the gift that each day truly represents. Many older couples I work with don't worry about the small stuff; they are just so freaking pumped to be healthy that whatever is going on is fantastic. They are always operating from the perspective of living above the clouds. They rarely waste energy on the storms, because a day with coffee on your pants is way better than no day at all.

What about when you were a child? Would food on your shirt or mismatched socks ruin your day? How worried were you about what others might think about you?

We can change our perspective before we are in our 80's or 90's. We can regain that youthful, carefree joy and laughter when things don't go right. We can decide not to take the easy road and get caught in the rain and dark clouds of life. We can rise above all the crap and enjoy the days and get as much out of them as possible by not rushing to get them over with.

Picture a bottle of water that has just a little bit left in it. Maybe one more sip will finish it off. You've gotten almost everything you can out of it, and it is so close to being empty. Next to it is another bottle that you just took the cap off of. The water almost flowing over the top. So much water still there. So much yet to drink.

Every day is like a bottle of water. The water represents the moments, the joy, the laugher, the experiences that make up the very fabric of our days. The bottle holds all of the possible life we can take in. Each day we are given a new chance, a new opportunity, a new bottle to live to the fullest.

When you look at it before you go to bed tonight, how much water will be left in the bottle that is today? Did you just race to get the day over with, or did you enjoy and drink up every drop? Did you take in and experience everything today had to offer? Is the bottle completely empty and everything that today could be, it was? Or, did you only take a little sip of today and barely experience any of it, because you were just trying to get through it?

When you start to look back at your life, what do the bottles from each day of your past look like?

Are there bottles from countless days still filled up almost to the top, or maybe you didn't even open them? Did you just go through the motions and not experience anything, not drinking up anything from so many days of your life so far?

When it's over, and you start to look back, how much of the water of your life is going to be left in the bottles? If you start to add up all the moments that were missed, all the days you rushed through, or days you didn't pay attention to, are there countless bottles with so much life left to live?

Do you start to see how many bottles there were from this past week, this month and even this year that are more than half filled, or never opened?

When your life is over, will there be so much water left over that you end up pouring everything of what could have been down the drain?

We need to drink up each day. We need to take it all in. We can't let the moments from any day or week get left behind.

Will all the bottles of your life look like an untouched crate in the warehouse at Costco with the plastic wrap still around them all?

Or, does yours look like it was a raging water party at a huge festival where all the bottles are empty, opened, and strewn all over the ground. Not a drop left.

Get drunk on the water of your life. Drink up the days. Get crazy about each bottle and crack open a fresh one each morning.

Think about each day and the bottle you are given.

Today is April 19, 2018. I'm going to party and drink up every ounce of what today could be!

Don't waste a single bottle. You can't go back and drink up the ones you missed, but you can make damn sure you don't leave any full ones from now on.

Drink it all up.

Leave nothing but empty bottles in your wake.

7 WELL ROUNDED

How often do you do something that makes your soul catch on fire? Has it been months, or even years since you had that feeling? Do you remember that energy, that emotion, the sensation of being truly alive from when you were younger? Where has that raw passion from when you were a child gone? For many of us, it faded little by little, so we barely noticed it going away. Bit by bit we sacrificed what mattered, and over time we forgot it was even there. For too many of us, it was because we felt that to please others or get ready for our future we had to put aside what we wanted or cared about. We gave up doing what we loved or were interested in, to do and be what others wanted for us.

Did you feel like you could be "you" growing up, or were you worried about meeting others expectations? Did you feel like you needed to act a certain way or do certain things to please others or your parents? Were there countless moments where you did what you knew your mom or dad wanted you to do, rather than disappoint them?

Are you taking the biggest leap possible whereby you truly honor the gifts that you have and share them with the world? What about your children? Do you ask them to move everything that makes them special into the background to fit in with they are "supposed" to be doing too?

Do we sacrifice or not even consider letting those desires of ours out, because we are too concerned with what we should be doing? When you were growing up did you feel like there was a plan for you? Were there countless moments where you did something more because of what you felt you needed to do, rather than what you wanted to do? Were you more worried about building your resume for life rather than living it?

How much time and energy do we put into things solely to fill up lines on a page for that next step? Are we constantly sacrificing today for the hopes of what it could mean for us tomorrow? Does the "best" college always lead to the "perfect" job and the "ideal" life? When do we finally stop putting all our focus on where we will be in 5 or ten years and start focusing on where we are today? Is it possible that living your life today may lead you to a better place in the future; rather than making all your decisions based on where you hope they might get you? When is the day that you finally decide that you are going to live for the present than for the future?

When do we start to let kids determine who they are and what matters most, when for much of their lives they are never given the tools to explore and open their minds to who they could be. Society, coaches, parents, teachers, and friends are the ones that tell them what they should do, what areas they are talented in, or what areas they need to work on to "improve themselves." Do we encourage them to really consider what it is that they want to do, find what they are passionate about, or what they want to spend their time doing?

You wanted to play lacrosse, but your dad grew up playing baseball. He always planned on coaching you, but all you remember hearing about is that you didn't play the sport he loves. You loved keeping your hair short, but your mom always wore hers long. You remember her always telling you how pretty it would look longer, rather than telling you how great it looks the way you like it.

As individuals, we aren't designed to like, enjoy, and most importantly be good at everything we do and experience. Yet we all seem to have an unrealistic expectation that we should all like and do the same things. We too often expect ourselves and even more so our children to be successful in all aspects of life, especially the areas that we are interested in too. "*I don't know why my child doesn't like _____, I loved it when I was their age.*" Many children feel the pressure and expectation of what they should focus on and who they are supposed to be. With social media and all the other ways they have to be assessed and evaluated, it may be tougher now than ever before to grow up.

They need to weigh a certain amount.

They need to look a certain way.

They need to drive a certain car.

They need to get a certain number of likes.

They need to play certain sports.

They need to get into certain schools.

They need to keep up with the latest trends.

They need to, they need to, they need to….

The list goes on and on and on. They are supposed to do it all and know it all.

As we grow up we are often only hearing about the other things we "need to be doing", rather than any interest being shown for what we are doing. Do you remember how limiting it felt to have to do things based on someone else's expectations? Did you have to take part in activities or sports because they were the ones that your parents wanted you to do or play? It goes without saying but imagine if the most brilliant – scientists, thinkers, artists, musicians, or athletes were told that they should spend more time on things they didn't like or weren't good at.

If, instead of what they have done and contributed to the world, they weren't given the time and opportunity to explore and develop their gifts and talents, but rather were forced to work on the other aspects of their life to become more well-rounded, build their resume, or to follow in their parent's footsteps.

Yea, Lady Gaga, I know you love to play the piano and sing, but you really need to work on your chemistry skills because that last volcano you made exploded and almost burned down the entire school. There was lava all over the roof and it ruined Timmy's water purification experiment. I know you don't like it, but we are going to send you to science summer camp. Once your work improves, we'll see if there is any time for the piano and singing.

Ryan Seacrest, last year on the football team you were the skinniest guy out there and we all thought you were going to die when that linebacker tackled you in the last game. We really worry you are going to get hurt this year. You can't just hang out at the radio station learning to be a DJ. I know you like doing whatever it is that you are doing when you sit and talk all day, but we are going to get you a personal trainer to start lifting and work on your footwork and route-running skills to get ready for the upcoming season. You need to start drinking protein shakes and need to be eating at least 3,000 calories a day to get ready for football.

Steve Harvey, yea you are pretty funny and people love your smile, but you need to get serious. Stop wasting your time, always trying to crack jokes and make people laugh. You are never going to make it in life as a comedian. You need to focus on getting a real job like everyone else. Life isn't about doing what you love, so you better give up on that dream of entertaining because that isn't realistic.

Were they celebrated for who they were and their unique talents and gifts before they became famous? Yes, we can see how great they are now, but did they get the same amount of support and encouragement before having sold out concerts, countless TV shows, or their own production company? Can we see individuals and encourage them when they are going through the struggle, or only when they make it?

Where would they be now and would the contributions they've made to the world still have happened? Or would they be stuck toiling away on something they don't enjoy or aren't good at?

These people stepped into life and shared who they were with the world. They didn't hold back. They blocked out what others said they should or shouldn't do. They were focused on what they loved, what they felt, and what they wanted to create. Mark Zuckerberg dropped out of Harvard, and you can bet his parents weren't happy.

They knew where their passions were and they unleashed who they were on life regardless of what anyone else said.

Is it possible that the next Pink, Ellen DeGeneres, Gary Vaynerchuk, or Kevin Hart could be worrying about not being good enough in a certain area of their life? That Kelly Slater, Emma Stone, or Macklemore could be stuck doing what their parents think they should be doing rather than what they want? That the worry is that they may fall behind others in certain areas and not be good at everything?

Did you discard the things in life you were truly passionate about somewhere along the way, to focus only on the things you were told you needed to improve in? Do we remember how that felt, yet continue the process for the next generation? Do we shift our own expectations, hopes, and dreams onto the lives of others? Does building the perfect well rounded child really lead to the end result we all think?

Are you forcing your child to practice basketball every day to get better because you know that is what they need? Do they really love it? Are they excited practicing and love the game, or is this about what you want for them? Does your child really want to become a lawyer? Do you tell them you will pay for college, but only if they study law because that is what you want, rather than what they are passionate about?

Where will they end up if they spend hours, days, and even years working away at something they don't have a burning desire for? Is your child really going to be good at basketball, or are they going to burn out in the 11th grade and never want to see a ball again? Is your teenager going to end up practicing law and spend every day feeling like she is living someone else's life?

Some of the most amazing contributions to the world and human existence have come because people were unapologetic about something. Who they were and what they loved.

What made their souls catch on fire. Their inner voice was not stifled, but shouted from the rooftops.

They didn't let themselves be forced into a box. The focus wasn't on them being everything, just themselves. Most importantly, they didn't care about what anyone else thought they should be doing, studying, or playing. What they cared about was letting the magic that they were born with come through them and be shared with the world. They knew that they had something to share. A song, a sketch, a dance, a joke, something that only they could do that needed to be given to the world.

It goes without saying that most of us may not have a spectacular talent. However, what happens when we take a closer look at our lives today?

Are you given the opportunities to be yourself? Are your children? Do we take the time to get to know who they really are and what makes them tick? Or is everything we think and see through the lens of what we think their life should look like? Do we ask what matters to them, and more importantly, what they want to do; or is the focus on them doing what we did, but only better because of our help? Are we repeating the frustrating patterns we dealt with because we haven't looked at it differently?

Is the goal for kids to be "well rounded" or to be real and be themselves?

This isn't about their grades in eighth grade. This is about their life. Yes, in grade school they can't just get all F's and one A. That isn't what is important. They need to study and learn as they grow up. Part of the beauty of life, though, is finding what subjects, what topics and what experiences make them come alive.

Is the goal for them to get C's in life and be okay at everything? Or to get one or two A+'s in the areas of life that they love?

"*My side hustle is paying off. I've been working on my t-shirt company on nights and weekends, and people are loving my stuff! The awesome comments I'm getting about my designs on my website is amazing!! This is so fun to see people getting me and my work!*"

You talk to them after yoga class and they say, "*I freaking love doing yoga! I love it!! I've been taking classes for months and am so pumped that I can do a headstand now.*"

"*Holy crap! I actually wrote the code for an entire new game and created my own app that people can play it! It worked!! This is amazing!! I can't believe it!*"

Have you allowed yourself to explore or find what you truly love? Has the goal been for you to do everything and be everything? If you could go back in time were there things you wish you had given more time to? Was there a passion you gave up on? Have you given your children that same freedom? Do you feel like the person who is getting C's at everything because you don't know what you are passionate about or haven't prioritized what matters most? Where would you be if you were given that support when you were younger? Would your life be different if you didn't do things because of others expectations, or because of what you felt your parents wanted?

Their gifts are there. Their talents are there. They have amazing things to share with the world. We need the version of them that is allowed and encouraged to share those skills. A child wants so badly to make their parents happy. Too often that is them doing things they know they don't want to do only to please mom and dad.

When you get to the end of your life you likely aren't going to look back with fondness at all the things you made them do to keep up with everyone else, build their resume, or to please you. You won't smile thinking about them looking miserable playing second base because you did, but you will never forget hugging them after they scored the big goal in their lacrosse game. You are going to remember what they created, what they made, their original ideas, what they shared, and how you helped them uncover their gifts.

Or, we can be caught up in the "Sheepification" of our own children. Worried about what they do and what that says about you. Worried about what the other parents will say if they don't do this or aren't involved in that. We can be confident enough in our own journey to not have to look behind to have our children following our same path. Instead, have the strength to get them out of our shadow. Helping them find their own way, and encouraging them to step out of the herd themselves, regardless of what the other sheep will say.

It's okay to focus on what you love. It's okay to share your gifts. Just as important is helping and encouraging others to do the same. It's never too late to allow them to be the amazing gift they are.

We can stop worrying about what others actions say about us. What your child does is not who you are. As a parent your ability to encourage your child to be the truest version of themselves will be one of the greatest gifts you can ever give them.

A true Blue Goat will never look back and see their children behind them. They will always be close by to help or protect them, but with pride they will look out to the fields and see them exploring and finding their own way.

8 CHECK THE BOX

The search for the idea of "happiness" and "success" has led us all astray from the more important goal.

We think of these terms, and it paints a certain picture. The picture just might not be the one that we take the time to create for ourselves.

We are all told the following:

Go to school. Be involved in everything from choir to student government, sports, and volunteer so you can get into a good college.

Get good grades in college and take classes and major in something that can get you a "good" job.

Get a good job.

Work hard to climb the corporate ladder and increase your pay and make more money.

Have a career, home, marriage, children.

Check the box, check the box, check the box, check the box and POOF!!!

HAPPINESS!!

"I'm dancing in the street I'm so freaking happy!! I absolutely love my life so much that I want to shout it from the rooftops and let the world know that my soul is on fire with life and joy! I am exactly where I want to be this very moment and wouldn't change a thing!"

Only that isn't what we say.

"It's more like. "My job sucks. My boss is an asshole who doesn't know my value. I'm stressed out about sending our kids to college and if I'm ever going to be able to retire. I feel like crap and know I'm 20lbs over-weight but don't have the time to work out, or even get a full night sleep. I can't make changes or quit now because I have a mortgage and everything else to take care of, so it is what it is."

How many people do you know like that?

Is this you?

How many people do you look at and without them even saying a word you can sense that they aren't happy. You can literally feel it. The energy they give off. The way they interact with the people and the world around them. You can see it in how they carry themselves, the way they look at you. The negativity, the frustration, the disappointment all boiling up just under the surface. You know at any moment they might explode.

Arms spread over their head, back arched, legs spread wide, like Lady Gaga's volcano they erupt….

"*AAAAAAAGGGGGHHHHHHHH!!!!*"

They are so pissed off at life, and they don't know why.

They snap because the checkout line at the grocery store doesn't move fast enough; they miss catching the elevator; the takeout order was wrong and they didn't realize until they got home, but they aren't really upset about that. They are upset about so much more. Deep down, they know they aren't where they want to be. Something is missing.

They've been checking the boxes all along just like they were told to and…nothing.

They don't feel any different, who they are hasn't changed, and they begin to feel the frustration of expecting a result from all the work and never feeling happy, never achieving the success that was supposed to come from it all.

We hope for an amazing outcome to our life, but give up control by listening to all the voices that tell us what our life should look like. We are told when and how we will find happiness, what it will mean to be successful, and what we should be doing to get there.

We need to take back control.

To live a life of your own choosing is one of the toughest tasks there is.

To uncover the most difficult truth and face it head on and live up to the challenge.

Checking a series of boxes in life isn't the ultimate goal.

How many times have you checked one of those boxes and have felt nothing?

Maybe it was a vacation you finally took, the new car with all the bells and whistles, the bigger flat screen, or getting your kitchen remodeled. For a few moments, you were really excited about what you had or what you could do.

But how did you actually feel inside?

Were you as a person, as you, fundamentally changed at all? Did the arc of the story of your life move in a new direction?

We forget that the only constant in the journey is ourselves. While the boxes that we check, or look to check may change, the only constant is that it is still us moving on our journey.

So, are we checking boxes for things and stuff, or are there possibly other boxes we can seek out?

The quest for some "thing" or some "one" to be the spark, the change, the impetus behind your move from not happy to happy is not the answer to the problem.

We are sold the story day after day and commercial after commercial that by having certain things in our lives those items will create the happiness for us that we so desperately seek.

Regardless of what the world tells you every day and tries to entice you to buy or do or change about yourself, nothing can bring you true happiness and contentment other than you.

Happiness is not an event based on checking off a box. Happiness is a state of awareness that the decisions you make are ones that honor the amazing person you are.

The biggest issue plaguing us is we are constantly looking for external factors to fix something that can only be fixed internally.

We never take the time to find out who we are and what matters; instead we listen to the world around us to tell us who we are and what matters. We are bombarded with messages of all the things we don't have and all the areas that we fall short in life. We wait and work and wait and work and do all the things to hopefully one day hear the world say to us "you are enough", "you've done enough", "you have enough", "you've made it", "you are successful now", but we never do.

We forget that it isn't anyone else's job to tell us those things.

It is your job to find the truth that, right now, you are enough. There can never be sufficient things or external markers to make you more than you already are.

If you don't feel that way about yourself, the only way to fix it is by looking in rather than looking out.

This begins our attempt and desire to find "happiness" by what we are told should fill us up and bring us joy rather than by finding that out for ourselves. Yet we are surprised that what others say we need doesn't give us the results and joy we so desperately want.

You are what matters.

What fills you up? What makes you come alive? Who do you want to be?

Too many of us never think about that stuff. We think about all the window dressing and shiny things, rather than about what really matters. We worry about what others have and if they are happy or not.

We are told and sold the version that we are supposed to have. It involves stuff and things.

So many people have all the stuff and so many things, yet they feel no different than they did before getting it all.

They realize too late that contentment is a concept that has been twisted from an introspective personal journey to the outward act of consumption.

So where does that leave us? Alone, with ourselves to find the answers to the questions that need to be asked.

What matters?

Not to anyone else.

What matters to you?

If you take away all the magazines, all the advertisements, all the media, your family's expectations, friends, what would you chose? How would you decide what to do with your time and what boxes would you be trying to check? Without the noise around you and others' input, would your goals be any different?

What moments in life are going to be the ones you look back on and truly care about checking off?

Checklist for Happy Life

Fancy Car ___

Marry attractive person ___

Big home ___

Huge wardrobe ___

Lots of money ___

Important job ___

Or…

Would yours look like this?

Great relationship with my children___

Career filled with passion___

Amazing marriage filled with love___

Fantastic friendships___

If you didn't check off any of the items on the list that life gives you would your life have any value? Would you be a failure in your life if you didn't have a nice car, big home and important job? Could you have a life of meaning and purpose and significance without those things?

We already know those check boxes don't work; they don't get us to where we want to be. They never have and they likely never will. I see it every day. I talk to people who have everything checked off the list, yet inside still feel the same way they did before all their "success".

You can create the boxes.

The blank sheet of paper is in front of you.

You can decide what the boxes are and create goals that are as unique as you are.

It's time to focus on the only goals that really matter. The ones that will fill you up, make you smile and bring true joy and emotion to your life.

We need to crumple up and throw the sheet of paper that life gives us in the trash. The one that everyone born is given that has the same boxes on it. The same one that has been given to everyone year after year.

Success in life is not something that you can seek out.

Success is not an outcome of checking the boxes life gives us.

Success is when you become the fullest expression of the amazing person you see in yourself and create your own boxes to check off.

Sheep care about checking the same boxes and moving along with everyone else in the herd.

Blue Goats don't give a bleat about any of that.

9 GOOOOOAAAAL!!!

Every moment of the day we are faced with decisions. Some of them are big, but many of them are so small that at first you may not even grasp they are happening.

When you were younger, you didn't wear your favorite Spiderman shirt because the bully in class who likes Wolverine was making fun of another kid for his Spiderman backpack. You were afraid he was going to make fun of you next.

Even though you freaking love Spiderman!

That younger version didn't realize it, but he just gave up a small piece of you in that moment. You let worry about what someone else would think or say keep you from doing something that made you feel great and told the world who you are.

In high school, you find that the cool kid drinks Diet Coke every day at your lunch table and even though you don't like Diet Coke and love Arizona Ice Tea you start ordering Diet Coke too.

You don't like Pilates and yet on a weekly basis you find yourself on the machine with your legs up in the air, thinking, "*What the hell am I doing? I don't like this at all.*" With sweat dripping off your face and your body contorted like a pretzel you look around, "*Everyone looks like they are really into this. "How much longer until we get the hell out of here!*" But all the other girls are doing it, so you don't want to miss out on being with the crew and hanging out with your friends for a post-class latte at Starbucks.

At work, you find out that all the guys wear a certain brand of dress shirts. You heard them giving the other new guy crap about his shirt, so the next day you go online and order new shirts rather than dealing with hearing trash talk about what you wear. The next week when you are sitting next to one of them in a meeting he looks at you, points with his pen at your pocket where the logo is and gives you a little wink and nod. You made the right call, right?

You make these sacrifices to be liked, fit in, and not be challenged for the even small things you care about.

What music you listen to. Who you date. What sports you play. Where you buy your coffee. What team you cheer on. Who you vote for. What fraternity you join. Where you live. What car you drive. How much you spend on your child's birthday. Where you vacation. What brands you wear. What you watch.

All choices. All seemingly small, but we forget that they all either lead us closer to who we are; or further away from who we are and could become.

You may begin to feel less and less like yourself and more like you are playing a role, acting out a character, or fulfilling someone else's expectations of you. Over time when you look in the mirror you may see someone looking back, but you might not know them. You've given up so much of who you are that when you really look at yourself, you aren't exactly sure of the person you've become.

We should look at this as being given hundreds, thousands, and millions of small choices. Each one an opportunity to be who we are; or slowly become someone else. So, what do you do with each one? Every moment is a chance to either chart your own course and make a life that is your own, or to allow other people's thoughts, wishes and, even worse, their crap, issues, insecurities, and negativity influence your decisions.

Being different and standing out for the sake of being unique isn't the goal. It's not about wearing a different shirt just because no one else is wearing it. It's about choosing to live where you want to live because you absolutely love the house and don't care if it isn't in the right neighborhood or where "everyone else" lives. It's not about drinking something other than Diet Coke just to say you aren't like everyone else. It's about drinking Arizona Ice Tea because you love the way it tastes and nothing else.

Each year all your buddies play fantasy football. You couldn't care less. Yet there you are spending hours researching, studying, watching ESPN and trading players because you don't want to be left out and get crap for not playing.

You actually love soccer.

It's not about playing fantasy football because everyone else does it, but watching soccer with your two friends that love it too and jumping off the couch and going crazy when your favorite player scores and the announcer yells "*GOOOOOOOAAAAAAL! GOAL! GOAL! GOAL GOAL!!!!*"

It's about being in those moments that make you feel alive. Not doing things because others are, or because you feel like you need to or should.

This isn't for the purpose of pissing others off and being difficult either. This is about so much more. This is about being able to look in the mirror and know exactly who is looking back at you. It's about finding the confidence to step out of the shadows, into the spotlight of who you know you are.

This is about finding that internal voice that gives you constant feedback about who you are and what you are doing. Not allowing who you are to slowly be lost moment by moment and choice by choice.

Take the time to listen to your inner voice and determine whether it is your soulful voice trying to help you make decisions that will lead you down the road less traveled and into the beautiful place that is "your life," or whether it is the voice coming from external forces like the media, a co-worker, teacher, friend, or society.

When you wake up in the morning, you know you are exactly where you need to be. We call where we live our "home," but we need to find the home that is in us. The place where, when you think about yourself, you only feel strength, comfort, stability, safety, and security. Like a tall oak tree with roots stretching deep into the ground you are unwavering in being you.

Who you are is the place you feel most comfortable because you are as real as you can be. Where you don't have to worry about doing specific things, acting a certain way, or showing up in the world as anyone other than yourself.

Who you are is knowing that the steps you are going to take are going to lead you where you want to be, not where you think you should be. It's what you choose to spend your time on, not what you think you are expected to spend your time on. It's knowing that when you lay your head down on the pillow at night, you will be smiling. You will sleep knowing that you are living your life as you, not as a character in a play.

When you wake up, you won't try to just get through the day, or "deal" with your circumstances, but rather live each moment, take each step with purpose. If you find yourself off track, you will know now rather than when it is too late.

When you sit down on your last day, whenever that is, you will be ready and be filled with joy and love and laughter, not regret, pain, and the feeling of a life that could have been.

Too many of us spend so much of our time and effort worrying and thinking about how our decisions will be interpreted by others. What others will think if we don't go along with the crowd. Blue Goats don't care what all the sheep are doing. They don't care about who is into what and what the latest and greatest thing is.

Blue Goats live with comfort and confidence that being themselves and choosing to do what they love is enough.

10 THIS IS IT?

Sometimes we don't really pay attention to time. It seems like we have so much of it ahead of us and so many things to deal with and "stuff" to get done that there will always be enough time. If anything, it may feel like the future can't get here fast enough.

Yet at the same time days, years, and even decades can pass in what feels like the blink of an eye.

When you get to the end of your life and you look back, what will you say?

What will you feel about the decisions you've made? It may not be your death bed; it could come before that. You don't know when you'll finally stop, look around and take notice of where you are and what you're doing with your one life.

Karl was in every way the picture of success. He had been a doctor for over thirty years and was retiring. As his financial advisor, I sat down with Karl to talk about the next phase in his life. I was excited to hear about what he was looking forward to and was anticipating his enthusiasm for the new chapter and the end of his working career.

Karl looked at me and said, "*I always thought it would be different.*" I asked what he meant and he said, "*I thought I would be excited to retire, but I honestly don't feel excited.*"

He went on to talk about how he had gotten to this point that so many before him had hoped to achieve and so many more still are fighting to get to, the finish line of his lifetime of work. Now that the years of grinding were done, he could retire and travel, laugh, sip wine and "finally start enjoying life."

Karl had worked his butt off. He had gone to a good high school and worked hard to get good grades. There were a bunch of doctors in his family, so he always felt a certain level of pressure to be like the rest of them and follow in his father's footsteps. He got into a great college and studied and worked and studied some more.

Karl graduated with honors. He then enrolled in med school and then it was more work, studying and then spending countless hours during his residency in the hospital. He fell in love and was married in his twenties. She was truly the love of his life. They were so happy back then, he said.

When he finally started his career as a doctor, it was countless hours, more work, and even less time with his wife. He said he enjoyed it, but in looking back it was more about fulfilling expectations and living up to what he was "supposed" to be doing than it was about making choices to do something he loved. Were there days he enjoyed being a doctor? Absolutely, but something was missing.

When he was young, Karl remembered, his dad missed his high school basketball games because he was always working. They never had a great relationship because his dad was always gone. His dad thought that the "stuff" from video games, new shoes, the big home, new bikes, and trips would make Karl happy, but he honestly just wanted to throw the football with his dad in the front yard or have him come to his basketball games.

The new cars, bigger home, and country club membership were now all part of Karl's life and he was successful in everyone's eyes. He just didn't feel like it.

Now here he was, making the same decisions and feeling the pain of a strained relationship with a son he barely knew. When he and his son did talk, he could feel the resentment. Without ever wanting it to be the case, or knowing how it happened, Karl had become his dad.

His wife was always great and supportive, but the spark was no longer there. The long nights and time apart was only made worse by their son graduating. They didn't have the bond of a child to keep things together.

So, they separated. Now, just over a decade later, here he is, turning sixty-four years old. For the first time in his life, he looked around and took stock of who he was and where he was.

"*What I realized is that my life is not at all what I thought it would be. I just never pictured this for myself.*"

He went on…"*I finally realized that my entire life I've been doing everything and making all of my choices based on what I thought would make others happy. Based on what I felt others would want me to do, what I was told to do, and even worse, what I assumed I was supposed to do. As a doctor, I obviously needed to drive a nice car; I had to have the big house, etc., etc., etc. None of it was my own doing. Yes, I bought those things, but I did them on the assumption that they would make me feel something or because I was supposed to. Everyone seeing that I was successful, making my parents proud, and being wealthy would be all I ever needed.*"

Only it wasn't.

Think back to when you were a kid. What did you love? What did you absolutely enjoy doing? What were the parts of your life that you couldn't do without? Do you see the things you gave up or didn't pursue? The Ice Tea you didn't have because you were too worried about drinking Diet Coke like the cool kid, or the Spiderman shirt you didn't wear for fear of the Wolverine-loving bully.

Have you been making decisions based on the wrong things for that long?

Karl was so far removed from that time in his life and what those pieces of him were that he didn't know how to start trying to find his way back to who he once was. When he looked in the mirror, he didn't recognize who was looking back. He was a shell of his younger self.

For much of his life he didn't pay attention or give two thoughts to the choices, purchases, and decisions he made, to the actions he took, because he was simply going along with what he figured everyone else thought he should be doing. When his dad called the membership director of the country club when Karl was in his thirties to help him join, he didn't push back. It was the next step. Joining the club was what his dad and friends expected him to do.

Karl didn't spend any time thinking about the benefits he would get out of joining. He didn't think about the extra hours away from his son his weekly golf outings with the guys would cost. He didn't even really like golf that much, but all his friends were members.

He got sucked into practicing to get better, spending nights hitting balls at the range, reading about golf, drinking at the club, and all the club gossip. Yet when he stripped it down to the simplest level, he didn't give a crap about any of it. After years of practicing, he realized that he really didn't like golf. Regardless, he spent hours at the club because the other guys were always pressuring him to show up at the events, play a round, or just have a drink with them.

It was a monumental waste of the precious moments that make up Karl's life.

He didn't care about any of it. It brought him no joy. Even worse, he didn't know what he could have been doing instead.

Did he like the guitar? Was he into sales and marketing? Would he love kayaking or listening to jazz? He literally didn't know. Did he even like bourbon, or did he just drink it because that is what his dad drank and what all the guys at the club drank?

All those things that make us unique. All those pieces of the world that we grab on to and say, "*YES, this is what fills me up!*" had been surrendered so long ago that he didn't even know what they had been.

And the parents that he had been working so hard to make happy? Gone. They had passed years before. The other doctors and members at the club he spent so much energy being like or keeping up with? They were dealing with their own lives and long gone from caring about what Karl was up to.

Karl finally began to realize that all those factors and people that he put so much stock in when making his decisions turned out to not care, not to be there, and completely uninterested in where he was now.

Karl was left holding the bag.

He was left with the harshest reality of all. That his one life; the only one he will ever have, was not his own. He had lived a life that wasn't based on him searching for his own meaning, finding his own way, listening to his inner voice, and channeling his own unique gifts to become Karl. He wasn't the fullest version of himself and hadn't given the world the gift of who he is. The world will never have the most amazing gift of all.

Karl.

Was he a great doctor? Absolutely. But, he will never know what he could have been, done, contributed, or shared based on his amazing talents and unique skills. He will never know how amazing a father he could have been. What the relationship with his only son might have looked like. What the joyful life of love and laughter he and his wife could have had. The fulfillment he could have found consulting, teaching or even running his own business.

He won't get to have any of those things because he was too worried about living out others' expectations of what his life should be. His one and only life.

Instead, he was a sheep. He allowed himself with very little pushback to get moved into the herd. He put his head down and simply followed what others told him to do.

When he finally stopped and looked up, he realized that he had absolutely no idea where he was or who he was. All he knew was that he literally didn't know what he had done with the last sixty-four years of his life. It left him in a place he never thought he would be. When he zoomed in, the blue dot was so far from where he expected it to be, he didn't even know how to start heading in the right direction.

All too often we allow everyone around us to tell us to just follow the yellow brick road, follow the yellow brick road, follow the yellow brick road. So, we do. We keep working and doing everything to get to the Emerald City. All our energy and time is spent going somewhere we are promised all our dreams will come true. Only after spending your entire life trying to get there do you finally look around and realize that it's all bullshit. The great Oz is nothing more than an old man behind a curtain.

It's not what we thought at all.

"*This is it, huh? I thought my life was going to be so different,*" Karl said.

You know if you are heading to the place you really want to be, or if you are stuck heading to The Emerald city to meet The Great Oz because that is where you are told to go.

You can decide if your life is what you want it to be, or you can allow life to happen to you.

You can choose to live and say, "*Yes! This is it!*"

Or, when all is said and done... "*Oh crap, this is it??*"

11 SEWER GRATE

Life throws a lot at us every day. Work stress, kids, exams, relationships, family issues, dealing with clueless strangers at the grocery store and finding the time to actually sit down and eat a meal.

We have so much that we have to deal with.

Our emotions are often just below the surface, and we can be so frustrated with the smallest things:

The driver in the car in front of you who doesn't see that the light just turned from red to green. "*GooooOOOOOOOOO!!!!! It's GREEEEEEEEN!!*" We yell in the car by ourselves.

The person in history class who won't shut up and always asks another question and another question. Then wants to tell everyone about some show they watched on the History Channel about the topic.

The jerk in line in front of you at Starbucks who takes forever and is rude to everyone behind the register and even gives you a nasty look for just standing in his general vicinity.

The pent-up frustration you carry from having such a disconnected relationship with your parents growing up. You get stressed and angry every time you have to read an email from them or have to talk to them on the phone.

The ripped guy at the gym who sits on the machine you are waiting to use and is too busy taking selfies and making duck faces into the phone that he doesn't realize that others are trying to work out too.

The world around us can impact how we think and what we feel every moment of the day.

So, in what way do we let all the stuff happening around us change who we are? Do we have the perspective to keep all the crap going on from affecting us?

If you walk through the streets of any major city, you will cross over more metal grates on the sidewalk than you can count.

There are all kinds of grates covering construction work, electrical wires, and the sewer below. Some of them are wide grates you feel like you can fall through, and others have so many lines and bars set so close to one another that you can barely see through them.

In how you deal with the world around you, what type of grate are you?

Some of us have grates with so many lines on them that almost nothing gets by us without affecting us. Whatever happens in the world around us gets caught and trapped by our thoughts and our emotions.

We are the grate that every single piece of trash, gum, cigarette butt, and spit gets caught on.

Every bad look from a stranger, annoying sound, stupid commercial, and bad meal affects us. Over time this can change how the grate looks and how the world interacts with it.

Is yours the grate covered in coffee cups, gunk, leaves, pigeon feathers and trash? Does everything from the world around you get snagged on you? Are the bars too close together and won't let anything pass through? Does everyone else's trash start to change who you are?

Do you "feel" differently because of what is happening around you, or do you realize that you can decide what does or doesn't affect who you are and how you live?

Across the street is a different grate.

As you approach, you can see that the bars are almost a foot apart and there are big wide spaces between them. The trash doesn't get caught; it goes right to the sewer below. Coffee cup? It may not even hit one of the metal grates and goes through to the trash. The sandwich wrapper, leaves, even the rain water? None of it gets collected and builds up. The grates are only designed to catch the really important stuff. If anything is going to get caught in the grate it is going to be a big deal. It is there to protect real things in life from falling into the sewer below. All the little stuff? It doesn't even hit the metal bars.

How often do you allow your grates to get really close together? How often does everything going on around you negatively affect you?

The dirty look from the guy in the store.

The meal that doesn't taste the way we expected it to.

The jerk in traffic that cuts you off.

Someone else's child acting crazy and not behaving in Target.

When things have an impact on us, it is almost always the trash. It's other people's bad attitudes, anger, frustration, worry, anxiety, sadness, and rudeness. All too often our grates are only catching the crap. We have our bars set so close together that any of the trash from the world around us else gets caught up in our grate and starts to gunk it up.

When someone helps you with your bag, gives you a compliment, let's you skip them in line, or gives you their seat, how do you react? Does that help clean off the grate, or do you keep all the gunked-up trash in your life regardless of anything good that happens? Do you ever let the crap in your life go, or is it always a part of you?

If you look at the two grates across the street from one another, you notice something amazing.

On one side, you see the grate that catches everything and that doesn't allow anything to go through and takes everything personally. Each bar is so close you could barely fit a pen through. You can see all the pigeon poop, dirt, grime, gum, leaves and how it has created a film of dirty water on top of the grate. As people get closer they notice a green slime has formed from the trash making the water moldy and it is slowly dripping down the corner of the grate to the sewer below. People walk around the grate because of all the stuff that has accumulated on it. They don't want to be near it and step in its mess.

You then watch as people approach the other grate across the street. A few steps away from it, they slow down. They notice that the metal is much more spread apart. "*Holy crap, that caught me off guard,*" one friend says to the other. "*You never see grates like that around the city.*"

They notice how clean it is because all the crap from the environment it isn't caught by the grate. The bars are set so far apart from one another. It is only focused on letting things that are really important affect it. It's not worrying about catching someone else's trash. Trash goes in the sewer below; that's the sewer's job. The grate isn't there to catch all the crap and stranger's filth. The people are amazed by what they see because they are used to seeing city grates full of everything. They know that if they fell, the grate would be there to catch them, but it's not going to catch any trash they drop. That's not the grate's job.

In the way you show up in the world are you only looking for the trash? Do you seek out the good and the positive moments, or is all your attention on what isn't right? Are your negative expectations constantly reinforced, because all you look for is what isn't as good as it could be?

What does your grate catch? Every little thing that goes wrong around you? Every little piece of trash from the people you care about, or even garbage from strangers?

Or do you let all of that pass right through without affecting you one bit? Do you stay strong knowing that if something real happens, you are there, but otherwise it isn't worth you collecting all the garbage? Your grate is too important to get clogged up with all the crap that the world will throw at you.

You can allow it to change you and how you interact with the world and how the world interacts with you, or you can know that all the B.S. out there isn't worthy of being caught by you, and you can let it go right where it belongs. With all the other trash into the sewer below.

Your grate is too important to be wasted and ruined by other people's trash. Your life and your energy are too valuable to let some person in line take anything away from the amazing day you are about to have.

Sometimes we just need to remember that we have the choice of how close we set up our grates. We control whether or not we let things affect us.

We can look and feel like all the garbage that has been dumped on us, or we can feel the light and free sensation of only paying attention to the serious stuff and letting everything else go.

The person you are will never be shared or seen if you let all the trash and crap bog you down. Let the sewer do its job. Let the trash go where it belongs while you feel the weightless joy of not being dragged down by the world around you.

Far too many people I meet with carry the weight of the trash that has accumulated on them over the years. Try to clean off your grate. See if you can remove the trash from the world around you. Move the bars around and set them farther apart. Let the little stuff pass right through you. As you stand there and interact with people, when you feel their trash coming at you, think of your body like the grate with the wide spaces. It flows right through you and into the sewer.

A Blue Goat will take the time to see if it has any trash on its grate. It will look to see if any garbage has been collected and needs to be cleaned off. It sees someone else's trash for what it is and can quickly determine what is real and what is garbage.

The real stuff gets the attention it deserves; the garbage in life flows right through to the sewer below.

12 WRONG RECIPE

The number of podcasts, books, articles, blogs, and presentations about how to be happier, skinnier, wealthier; ...ier,…ier,…ier,…ier is mind numbing. We are all looking for answers to everything in our life that isn't measuring up.

How can I be successful and wealthy?

How can I make my marriage work?

How can I be happy?

How did they get so many followers on their account?

Our society has spent billions of dollars trying to help us answer these questions. But we are looking at it all wrong. We analyze, interview, test, question, and review others' lives and what led them to success. What made them lose the weight? How did they get rich? We read the books, listen to the tapes and follow the instructions.

You don't get the job. The relationship ends. You are struggling financially and not successful.

Why?

What the hell went wrong? You know that you followed the steps. You know that you filled out the forms and read the manual, so why hasn't it worked for you? You listened to every podcast possible, but still nothing.

Because it shouldn't. It's not going to. It won't.

Not that way.

Trying to following the exact roadmap that led to someone else's success is not the answer.

You are not them and you aren't supposed to be. You aren't like anyone else.

Why would we take the recipe that made the perfect dinner for one chef and think it will taste the same with completely different ingredients?

We assume that the goal is to make a dish that has five ingredients. Eggs, flour, sugar, butter, water. Stir in bowl, heat for forty-five minutes at 450 degrees and presto cake! (I honestly don't even know if that makes cake, but you can look it up.) The point is that you are diligently following a recipe, but life doesn't call for recipes.

The issue is that you aren't making something simple like cake. Life isn't that cut and dry.

The next time you are in the grocery store, take a moment and pause when you first walk in.

As you start with the fresh produce section, look around at all the options and colors. There are fruits and vegetables in every shape and size. Sweet pineapple, fresh blueberries, and different types of apples. Kale, asparagus, pears, avocados, beets, green beans, tomatoes, and countless others.

You walk by the deli section, which has all the staples like turkey and ham, but now there are all kinds of smoked, glazed, spiced, and organic options. Not to mention the salami, capicola, prosciutto and other fancy meats.

You look at the dairy options and there is cheese from all over the world. You can get it in blocks, slices, grated and even blended. Almond milk, hemp milk, coconut milk, one percent milk, two percent milk, one-half percent milk, chocolate milk and all kinds of cage-free, free-range and caged-egg options.

Walking down the various aisles, you see thousands of choices in different bags and boxes for every palette. No fat, low fat, gluten free, egg free, sugar free, and of course the normal stuff.

You come to the spices. Ginger, cinnamon, cardamom, cloves, nutmeg, red pepper, black pepper, white pepper, thyme, basil, oregano, rosemary. And on and on. There are dozens of spices and herbs to add flavor to a meal.

The frozen food section adds countless more items and options from entire meals to desserts.

Now imagine if I told you and one other person to go to the same grocery story. You each had to pick out twenty items and five spices and make a dish.

As you walk around with your cart you can pick whatever twenty items you want. It doesn't matter at all.

You organize your items in the order of your choosing and simply pick which is item number one, item number two, item number three and so on.

Both of you are given the same recipe.

The instructions for the dish explain how much to use of each item.

One cup of item one. One tablespoon of item two. One half cup of item three.

The only issue is that your item one was shredded mozzarella and the other person's item one was gluten-free granola.

Their item two was pancake mix and your item two was frozen peas.

Their item three was salami and your item three was bananas.

As you continue to follow the instructions for each of the items, how different might the meals taste?

We may put the same amount in, every item measured perfectly, but we are using different ingredients. Yet we expect both dishes to smell and taste exactly the same.

You read about how Mark Cuban made millions in the tech industry so you listen to everything he has ever done, hear him speak and watch every episode of Shark Tank, yet your company doesn't get off the ground.

You research and follow how Sara Blakely started her company SPANX, but can't figure out why your business idea is struggling.

You read up on how Dwayne "The Rock" Johnson trains and what he eats. You follow the steps and yet look nothing like chiseled statue in the blockbuster movies.

How many times are we disappointed because we think by following the same recipe as someone else we will have the same outcome? Yet we hardly ever do.

We forget that we are not working with a handful of items from the grocery store and trying to make the same dish. When it comes to you and your life, it is far more complex than that.

There are infinite differences between you and whomever you wish to follow or emulate. In the very design of who we are, we are simply not the same. So why would we follow someone else's instructions for what worked for them and be surprised that it doesn't work for us?

We need to change the complete paradigm as it pertains to trying to mirror or emulate others. Following others' recipe for your own meal is going to lead to a shitty dinner.

You aren't anyone else. You shouldn't be.

Stop using other people's recipes to make your own dish.

Those people that you are following blazed their own trail. They maybe took inspiration from this person and a few ideas from that person, but what made them work, what made them stand out, was that they were themselves and lived their own life. They used their gifts. They didn't give a crap about what someone else created or what someone else wrote. They focused solely on what they wanted to create, what they wanted out of life and what they needed to share. They let their gifts come out. They focused on what they had going on in their soul and what they knew in their heart they had to do. They didn't worry about following a script, listening to a process, or going through the steps that worked for someone else.

They didn't follow the path. They didn't get behind a leader. They trusted their gut. They put in the work. They hustled. Most importantly, they let every bit of who they are and the amazing ingredients that made them up come out. They put every ounce of themselves on full display.

That is why they made it. That is why they were successful.

Not because they followed someone else's process. They created a new dish that was all their own, and the world absolutely loved it. The world had to have this new dish.

They were their own brand.

A new recipe that was unlike any other.

A gift that was the person and the expression of the perfect mix of ingredients that only they had.

You have that same opportunity. Your ingredients have never been shared before, and your gifts have never been on full display, so no old recipe can be used to get the most out of who you are.

Instead, you should create all new dishes, all new recipes, based on your amazing ingredients.

Like a chef that has his garden and all kinds of food to choose for his evening meal, you should look at and explore what can be harvested in your life. Look at the different parts of the garden, see what is ripe and what needs more time. Maybe there are parts of you that are blooming at this point in your life, and maybe there are parts that aren't ready. You will only know if you pay attention, look at who you are and see what gifts you have that should be the ingredients to your amazing life that no one else can make.

It's time we stop looking externally for guidance and start looking inward. You have all the ingredients you need to make a dish the world has never tasted.

We can keep eating shit sandwiches in life, or step into the kitchen of you, look around at all the possibilities and make something amazing.

If you look closely at the herd, do you see anything that stands out or grabs your attention?

It's time to shift your focus from being the next Beyonce, John Grisham, or Kardashian and spend your attention on being the first you.

13 CO-PILOT

It's been there since the beginning. You've heard it so many times before. Sometimes you listened, but all too often maybe you didn't.

Your personal co-pilot.

That voice inside your head is one of the greatest gifts you have. It is your personal compass and life guide. It knows what is best and where you should be going.

It knows what makes sense and what is in line with the life you are capable of and thus, what decisions will lead you in the right direction.

If you don't hear the voice, you likely haven't been listening for far too long. It is sitting there with all the maps to help you get to where you want to go. It is constantly giving you insight, thoughts, tips, ideas, and guideposts for what you should be doing. How to honor yourself and make the best decisions for your life.

The issue is that our co-pilot's voice is constantly being talked over by much louder voices blasted from huge speakers. Your co-pilot can be subtle. If you don't pay attention, the much louder voices of co-workers, relatives, friends, society and the media can drown it out. We have to learn to put on noise-canceling headphones and listen to the only voice that really matters.

Our own.

The longer you allow that inner voice to be drowned out by all the other noise from the world around you, the harder that voice is to hear.

The less you pay attention to it, the more likely that voice will stop talking to you.

All your girlfriends already bought the newest pair of jeans that have been all over Instagram and on the latest fashion blogs. After being asked multiple times why you haven't gotten them yet, you finally cave and sit down on your computer and decide to order them.

Your co-pilot says, "*What the hell are you doing?? We can't afford those! You already have five pairs of jeans and those new ones aren't even the type that flatter our butt! They are going to make us look squatty, and we are already stressed about our savings account. Don't do it!*"

You hear it. You know the truth. Yet you justify it. You come up with a reason, an excuse. "*I've seen these all over my news feed,*" you tell yourself. "*I've been working so hard the past few months I deserve to treat myself,*" or "*I don't want people to think I'm not fashionable like the rest of my friends.*"

You add them to your cart, you add the size you think you need and one other just in case the fit isn't what you expect.

The voice gets louder. "*What are you doing? I told you we don't need them!*"

Your credit card information is auto-filled and as you move your mouse over the *Complete Purchase* button, your co-pilot is looking right over your shoulder.

"*Don't you do it, don't you do it!!*" it says.

You bite your lip, knowing you shouldn't. You close your eyes and push down your finger.

"Click."

Purchase Complete

Your co-pilot smacks its head and falls back into the chair, exhausted.

"*WTF?!!?...*" it says.

You know it's there, you know your co-pilot was right, but you let outside voices like your friends, the media and social pressure drown out the only voice that mattered. Your own.

Or...

You listen to that inner voice and decide that you have plenty of jeans already and don't need to buy a new pair just because they are the newest thing and all your friends have them. You look at your checkout cart with the two pairs of jeans. Think about it for a quick second and say, "*You know what? I really don't need them. I love that pair I bought a few months ago, they make my butt look amazing anyway.*" You close your laptop and start working on dinner.

Your co-pilot says "*YES!! That's right!! Damn straight!!*" as they do a little butt dance and celebrate. They dance around your head and feel the joy and freedom of choosing what matters and what is important to you.

So instead of falling victim to the trend of the moment and adding stress and worry to your financial life you listened to your co-pilot. You made your decision based solely on what you want and need and didn't let all the other noise make the choice for you.

The longer you don't listen and chose option A, the quicker your co-pilot becomes disillusioned and decides it's not even worth saying anything because you aren't going to pay attention anyway.

Co-pilot? Some people say, I don't get those "gut" feelings at all.

Do you know why?

When your co-pilot has given you guidance, advice, and insight over and over and you failed to listen, it just gave up. After seven years, sixteen years, twenty-five years or more of you not listening, your co-pilot said:

"The hell with it. You never listen to me, so why even tell you what to do anymore. I've been trying to help you for over a decade, but you keep listening to everyone else, everything else, so you're on your own now."

So now your co-pilot is lying on the couch with a bowl of Cheetos binging on Netflix because it doesn't have anything else to do. It isn't listened to, isn't needed, and doesn't bother giving you guidance for your life.

The good news is that the relationship can always be repaired.

It might take time to get your inner voice to a place where it speaks up loudly, and where you realize that it truly is trying to put you on the best track, giving you guidance out of love. You just have to listen.

The baby steps of listening and acting upon the feedback you are given can slowly allow that co-pilot to regain its energy and desire to be your guide. If you listen closely enough, it may turn off *Orange is the New Black* and put down the Cheetos and get back to guiding.

It may be as simple as something like the food you eat. You keep thinking, "*I'm going to eat better.*" Every time you are about to order the bacon cheeseburger it says, "*What the hell!?!? I thought we were going to eat better!!*"

You hear that voice. You know it is there. Ordering the burger or not ordering the burger isn't just going to affect your weight and health.

The bigger impact is that you are taking the most powerful gift of self-guidance and your beautiful gift of self-awareness —and not listening.

It's not just about being in better shape or not buying new jeans. It is that every moment that you get those messages, they are coming for a reason.

Why don't we listen to those messages, the comments, the insight? We know we are telling ourselves things for a reason, but we listen to everything else.

Karl was getting those messages, over and over and over.

"*Do we really want to be a doctor?*"

"Why are we joining this country club; we don't even like golf!?"

"Wrap up this patient and get home, you already missed dinner!"

Yet he let friends and family tell him what to do, society tell him what to join, and work expectations tell him what he should do with his time. Year after year of this and his co-pilot gave up. Karl wasn't worried about getting to the place he was supposed to. He was okay going where all the other guides thought he should be.

There is an amazing life you could be leading and a guide trying to take you there.

Listening to your co-pilot and your inner voice is part of finding your path. What would change if you could block out the noise from the world around you and turn up your own volume? If you don't have a name for your co-pilot, it's time to get your relationship back on track.

If you pay attention, it is there all the time. You just have to listen.

Your feelings are the gift of self-guidance and direction.

There is a reason you are telling yourself certain things.

It's time to find out why.

14 GOLDEN EGG

How many times in life have you assumed and expected things to be a certain way, but when you got something or reached some milestone the reality was totally different?

We expect that by getting the new job, buying the new car, getting married, or making more money that our life would have new meaning, a new emotional tone, or we would experience a breakthrough or even feel complete. Not only was the result not as good as we expected, but often we were let down or felt even worse when those events happen.

We expend so much of our energy and effort to get or have things that we are told to go after in life.

For so many kids Easter morning is one of the best holidays because of the fun hunting for the eggs.

As you walked out the back door to start the hunt, there were countless eggs all over the place. So many that you could see in clear daylight! A blue one right there next to the tree. Oh, wow! A yellow one on the flowers and a pink one right there in the grass! The anticipation of getting all the eggs made your little legs run in place. The nervous energy made you swing the empty Easter basket back and forth in front of you from the excitement.

Just before you start, your parents tell you; "*There is one egg that is different from all the others. There are blue, pink, yellow, and green plastic eggs, but there is one special Golden Egg. There is only one, and whoever finds it will win the Easter egg hunt!*"

"*Go ahead!!*"

Off you go. Running over the grass and grabbing the yellow one on the flowers and the pink one right off the grass. Your heart starts beating faster, and your little legs run from egg to egg. As you grab each one you don't open it, you don't look to see what is in it, and before your hand can even drop it into the basket you are off looking for the next one. You want to get a bunch of eggs but also want to get the Golden Egg.

You run around the bushes and stop. You look over, and there is your brother with a basketful of eggs, but more importantly you lock eyes because right between you both is the Golden Egg. It was hidden behind a sprinkler head and could only be seen if you walked around behind the bushes; otherwise, it was blocked from your view.

Your brother takes off and an instant later you start running for it too!

You both are bounding towards it with all your effort, you hear eggs falling out of your basket from your frantic running, but you are too focused on the Golden Egg and winning to stop and pick them up, or worry about losing them.

Your hand grasps the metal foil of the shiny egg and you can feel their hand almost immediately cover yours. You pull back with all of your might, you turn and lift the Golden Egg high above your head and shout, "*The Golden Egg!! I found it! I won!!*"

This is the big prize. You've won the Easter Egg Hunt! You may have lost some of the plastic eggs along the way, but you got the Golden Egg.

You sit down and look at it. You marvel at the gold shimmering exterior and how pretty it looks. The metallic paper shouts success compared to the other eggs in your basket below. It's not like the other ones that are plastic and have a few jelly beans or candy in them.

The morning light hits the shiny exterior and you are so excited about your egg and can't wait to enjoy the sweet taste of success.

The first few pulls on the wrapper of the golden foil start to reveal the amazing chocolate coating. You can smell the sweetness of the milk and sugar and you anticipate the splendor that is yet to come. Mouthwatering, you pull back the gold wrapper and the perfect chocolate egg sits in your hand waiting for you to taste the spoils of winning. You start to feel a thin layer of chocolate melting on your fingers in the warm morning sun.

You put the entire egg in your mouth and brace for pure bliss.

You begin to taste the first hints of chocolate, and then you bite down to feel the chocolate break apart and some thick, gooey, warm, liquid oozes into your mouth.

EEEEEWWWwwwwwww!!!! GRRROOOOOOOOOSSSSSS!!!

You can barely get the words out. You have a mouth full of some snot-like substance and shards of the broken chocolate coating. The texture and the flavor make you gag and you look around for a place to spit it out.

Your lower lip drops as you try not to taste any of it and your mouth hangs open looking for a place to remove the edible taste of disappointment.

You try to get all of it out of your mouth and quickly open one of the blue plastic eggs to find a few jelly beans to devour to get the taste out.

You think back to all the work and energy put into getting the Golden Egg, when at the end of the day you are stuck with a nauseating mouthful of crap. Even as a kid, you feel fooled.

The distraction of the shiny goal kept you from enjoying the egg hunt. You didn't even take a moment to figure out what was in the Golden Egg at the very beginning.

Was it caramel filled? What it peanut butter flavored? What is a marshmallow? Was there money inside?

No, you just knew that it was the Golden Egg and that you were told that finding it was the goal.

It never occurred to you to find out what it was you were told to go after or what you would get for winning.

Even worse, had you known all along that it was a chocolate egg filled with a gelatinous goo you could have decided not to even look for it, because you love jelly beans.

You could have taken the same amount of time and effort and searched for the eggs that had exactly what you wanted, and when you found those eggs enjoyed the taste of success with each burst of juicy fruit flavor in your mouth.

When you are told to go after the Golden Egg, do you do it because you are worried someone else might get it first and take what you want? Or do you simply go after it because someone told you that was what you should be doing?

Having a mouthful of crap that you can spit out on an Easter morning doesn't compare to what you are left with when you finally realize that you've spent so much time, energy, and effort on getting the Golden Egg in life only to find it wasn't at all what you thought it was.

There are so many Golden Eggs people tell us to go after.

As life continues, we are constantly told about the next Golden Egg we should be chasing.

"As soon as you make partner, your life is going to be amazing!"

"I know this isn't in your price range but this home would change your life!"

"If you upgrade to this year's model you will really see what driving is all about."

"You will absolutely love cooking as soon as you remodel the kitchen!"

Every year the Easter Egg hunt happens, and each year we are fooled into chasing after and trying to get the next Golden Egg.

When someone tells you to go after the Golden Egg, you have to remember to ask the simplest question "Why?"

Without knowing why you are searching for something, or what that something is, you might spend all your time and energy going after something that, when you finally get there, you realize you don't really want after all.

Sometimes it's the plastic eggs filled with jelly beans that are really what we love. We just have to sit back and let everyone else in the herd chase the Golden Eggs.

15 WHAT IF

Fitting in.

Standing out.

Being different.

Failing.

Fear plays such a role in our lives and the decisions we make. How does fear keep you from doing the things you love? From spending your time differently? From working where you want to work and even drinking what you want to drink?

What are you afraid of in your life? What your friends will think if you do something different or don't go to the bar with them? That your boss will hate your idea? That you will get dumped if they find out you aren't a real blonde?

How many times have you let fear or worry determine your actions?

What are you giving up?

Do you not get to listen to music that makes you want to dance and sing? Do you have to go to a place and eat food you hate? Are you living somewhere that you can't stand? Is your relationship or job one you are settling for?

Or is it your own fear? Is it fear of being alone? Fear of losing the job, or not being invited to the party? Fear of losing the deal or missing out? Fear of being broke or upsetting others?

For many of us, fear comes from being where we know we shouldn't.

You are worried about breaking up and being alone. You don't want to be single and have to deal with going back into the dating pool and starting over again.

But that might not be the real fear.

Deep down, your co-pilot has been telling you for months that the relationship is no good. You two aren't meant to be together. You don't even like them that much.

The fear isn't about being single; the real fear is knowing you are in a bad relationship, but not doing anything about it.

You know you should break up, so, why don't you? You allow yourself to stay in a crappy relationship when you know deep down that it isn't what you want. It doesn't make you feel great. Yet you stay anyway.

Why am I letting myself stay in this terrible relationship? What am I doing?

You aren't worried about passing the history test. That isn't the real fear. Deep down, you are scared as to why you won't sit down and study when you know you should.

You know you will eat sweets if you have them in the house yet you keep buying them. You are worried about the fact that you eat them, but deep down, you are more scared about why you would self-sabotage and keep buying them in the first place.

Why do we let ourselves make decisions when we know we shouldn't?

The reality of knowing that we should be making certain decisions but aren't is also a huge reason we have so much fear in our lives.

As a result, we make decisions that begin to create a life that is much scarier than it should be. We don't value our time, we don't value our emotion, we don't value our worth and thus we make decisions that take away from what our life could look like.

You can feel the days, weeks and even years of your life slipping away as you work in a job that you hate. You can feel your life wasting away, yet you don't do anything about it. You can hear your co-pilot saying "*what the HELL are we doing?!?!? Get us out of here!! This sucks!!*" Yet you stay. You know the future version of yourself is sitting there pissed off at you for staying in the job and not getting to the next job where you will really flourish and grow.

Your co-pilot knows that every day you don't go to the gym you aren't getting in better shape. You create fear and worry about what that means in your life and what it means about your ability to take the hard step and start caring for yourself. Deep down you start to worry if you even think you are worthy of a great life or not.

You create excuses, reasons, even an alternate reality to what is really happening, but deep down you know the truth.

It leads to other decisions that aren't in line with what you know you should be doing.

In working with so many parents I've heard more stories that I can remember that go something like this:

You don't like your job and want to be making more money. You want to be able to provide more for your family but you haven't gotten a pay increase in a few years. Online, you keep seeing all the trips it seems like every other family is taking so you decide to do it. You book the trip using your credit card even though you know you can't afford it. You've been promising the kids you will go see Mickey Mouse at Disneyworld and at least this way others will see you as the parents that took your family on a special trip. You say to yourself, next month we will tighten things up and pay everything off. Only you don't. Now you start to worry and stress out about how you are going to manage getting the credit cards paid and dealing with your finances next month.

Now you are in a job you hate with growing credit card debt. Stress, frustration, worry, all of which come from choices. Those countless decisions we make. The result depends on whether we are making the ones we know we shouldn't, or paying attention to our co-pilot and doing things we know we should.

What if you could tap into that fear? What if you could look it in the eye and see where it is coming from?

Am I really scared that I won't find a new job? Or deep down am I more freaked out that I know I hate what I'm doing yet I stay anyway?

Do I have huge hopes and dreams of what I want my life to look like? Do I make vision boards and talk about the company I want to start and the places I want to go but never do?

Where does that leave me? Am I concerned about the new company failing, or am I more worried that I'll never have the nerve to even try?

Am I thinking that when I'm older I'll look back and everything will have been different than I had hoped or thought it could be?

Am I worried that the cute single person across the bar is going to reject me, or that I won't even have the nerve to go talk to them?

When you look back at all the worry, stress and fear in your past, how much of it has helped?

What if you let that all go? What if you realized that you don't need worry and you don't need fear.

What if you weren't concerned about getting dumped, losing the big deal, getting married?

What if you realized that if you are one hundred percent you in any situation, you shouldn't worry about the outcome?

You date someone and you are one hundred percent yourself, you give the relationship everything you have and they dump you. That is fantastic! It really is. That means that you were genuine. You were the most real version of who you are and the gifts you have and it just so happened that one person didn't see you as the person they wanted to be with.

That means that you know very simply that you shouldn't be together. You were you. You were real, honest, and true to who you are and gave it everything you had. It wasn't a fit. It's not that something is wrong with you. It's just that you weren't meant to be with that person.

It sounds so simple, but that is an amazing outcome! Why are we so afraid of that being looked at as failure? If you take a job and work hard and pour yourself into it and you don't have great success, or get fired, that doesn't mean you suck. It doesn't mean you are stupid. It means you shouldn't be doing that job. That is what life is about. It's not about trying to fly under the radar, getting by, or doing just enough. It is about being unapologetic about going after goals, relationships, and work. It's about being naked, vulnerable and open to whatever life throws at you, because the alternative is not living.

Most people are so worried about "failing" or "looking stupid" that they don't do anything. They are always the ones who are first to point out when things don't work out for others because they are the ones who don't have the balls to try anything in the first place. They are the Couch Cowards. They sit around and tell everyone else what they should or shouldn't do but don't have the courage to do anything themselves. They are always yelling from the sideline but never sweating and hustling in the game themselves. The Couch Cowards find comfort when things don't work out for others, when relationships fail, when life doesn't work out the way we hoped. It gives them comfort in staying exactly where they are. Going nowhere, right in the middle of the herd.

You know who they are; you always know they are there. The people who are more worried about throwing trash on everyone else's grates and telling others what they can or can't do. They are more concerned about things possibly not working out, than they are about seeing what they are capable of. Don't worry about those people, because nothing is going to change for them. You know where they will end up.

Experiencing life isn't going to come from being fifty percent into a project or sixty-five percent in a relationship. Joy results from you being completely yourself, authentic and real.

Too many of us only want to allow the good things that happen in life and are petrified of what it means if something isn't going well. We forget that what happens is not who we are. We are always the same person whether we are selling our company or falling in mud in front of strangers. Yet we are so petrified of the fall into mud that we don't live in a way to create the company.

You can't have it both ways.

Let others in and let yourself out. Failing is okay. Embarrassment is okay. Being totally heartbroken is okay.

I would guess that a broken heart mends differently based on the situation.

If you gave one hundred percent and were you and it didn't work out, how easy is that to walk away from? If you gave some of yourself, tried to be who you thought the other person wanted you to be, acted the way you thought you should, and did the things you expected they would want and it doesn't work, how frustrating is that? How many days, weeks and years are you going to pine over what could have been? "*But they didn't even know the real me*," you think to yourself. "*I can change; I can be different*," but it's too late.

Being the most real version of you possible will let you love more deeply and feel less pain. It may sound crazy, but when you are the truest version of yourself, there is an amazing power that comes from it. Fear comes in when we act and live like someone we think we are supposed to be, and it doesn't work out.

What if we stopped being so worried about what we think it says about us if things in life don't work out the way we expect and we "fail" at things?

What if you change your perspective and realize that every relationship isn't going to end in marriage. Every painting you do isn't going to be amazing. Every proposal you create isn't going to wow your boss. That is okay. That's exactly how life is supposed to be.

If you are 100% you, if you are 100% in, and 100% true to who you are, then there is no failure, only important lessons along the journey. The job doesn't work out, you don't hit your sales goals and you are let go. That isn't failure if you gave it everything you had. Rather, that is a great success, because you realized that you shouldn't be doing that job. As a result, you could move on, find the next job and get one step closer to the role that will allow you to truly shine. When you are 100% yourself in the right job you will see your skill, ability, and talent on full display and you will truly flourish in every way possible.

Instead, most of us are fearful of what the outcome might be so we don't give it our all. We act like the person we think the other person wants us to be. We do what we think our parents would want. We handle the sales pitch like we think our boss would want. We give it seventy-five percent because that way if it doesn't work out you always have in the back of your mind, "*I could have done more and I would have been successful.*"

We worry more about trying to get C+'s in everything we do rather than having a relationship that was a total F. Having a job that was a F-. Those are great outcomes. You find out what you did or didn't like about how the person made you feel, what you loved about certain parts of the job, and now you can look for those things as your journey continues.

Otherwise, you are trying to just make everything in life work out okay, or worse, hoping and wishing that if you don't give it all of you, then it leaves room for improvement or an excuse to fall back on.

Giving yourself that out is not honoring who you really are. You should be open to a relationship that ends in failure, okay with rejection. If you spend two years in a relationship trying to be the person your partner thinks you should be or you think they want you to be, how does that honor the amazing person you are? How many relationships like that end well? In being yourself, you will also find out much more quickly if the other person is a good fit for the real version of who you are. We keep trying to make every relationship work every time, rather than seeing them for what they are. Each relationship is an opportunity to either find your true love or to learn more about what you don't want in a partner.

We are all too worried about making every piece of the puzzle fit perfectly. We forget that we aren't made that way. We have unique features that make us up, ones that are different from so many others. Those are the best parts of you that when shared will attract the job, the friends, the spouse and the people you need in your life.

If you keep thinking to yourself, "*Why don't I have the spouse, house, and blouse I want!?!?*' You might need to realize that you haven't become the real 100% version of you that is ready for those things yet. You keep wondering why relationships aren't working out, why you keep dating the wrong people, why you don't live where you want to live, or don't have the wardrobe you want. Look in the mirror and determine if you are being yourself or not. Are you being the version of you that is wearing a mask or playing a role? If you are still acting and living like the person you think you should be, then you will attract the wrong people. Being you, being real, being genuine will finally turn over a new leaf that will draw the people that want to be with you rather than the people that want to be with the made-up version of you. In acting like someone else, you will find the people that are attracted to that version. It will leave you frustrated and upset as to why the wrong people keep showing up. If you are yourself, and you attract someone, the outcome will be far different because they are attracted and interested in the real you.

If you don't show up one hundred percent in life you will always be left wondering what could have been.

Be you. Share your gifts. Do it 100% the way that honors who you are and not who you think you should be.

Knowing that you aren't where you need to be and searching for your blue dot is where real courage is.

It's time you flip the fear in your life into curiosity. Find power and strength by stepping into the real you.

One will never find who they are in a place where everyone else has already been. A true adventure is going where no one else has traveled.

In being you there is no fear, no failure.

Only the joy of experiencing love, loss, and life in the most real way possible.

16 YES, TO YOU

Some of the easiest decisions that you ever face are the ones that are yes or no. There isn't that frustrating gray area that so much of our lives gets lost in.

"*Do you like anchovies? No.*"

"Do you want a cup of coffee? Yes."

The harder part of life is that over time we begin to realize that all too often we end up choosing both, saying yes and no at the same time.

Tim's mom asks if you can help and volunteer for the science fair at your child's school. You are super busy and absolutely hated science and still feel uncomfortable when your son asks you for help on his homework because you don't understand it all, but you don't want to feel bad and have the other moms think less of you so you say yes.

You feel like if you said no, there would be all kinds of negative repercussions. Bad looks at the next soccer game, whispers when you wait in line to pick your son up at the carpool lane. You've heard those conversations between the parents and know how mean they can be. You can just hear the comments about you not wanting to help, being lazy, not caring about the kids, etc., etc., etc.

So, you decide to do it, not because you want to help or are excited about the fair, but because you feel like you should. You are more worried about what happens if you don't say yes than you are about what saying yes will do for you.

How often do you allow decisions like this to be made almost on your behalf? You can hear your co-pilot telling you differently and you know you don't want to do it, but you say yes anyway.

What you may not realize is that by saying yes to helping and volunteering at the fair you really said no, just not to Tim's mom. You said no to the extra time that would have given you to spend with your child, catch up on your research, do yoga, finish your work presentation, read, run errands, or do whatever it is that is an outward expression of how much you value yourself and your time. You said no to honoring what you find important in your life and what you want to do with the moments that make up each day.

Most importantly you once again said no to your co-pilot. It wants you to say "*Thanks, Alice. I'd love to help, but right now I'm not adding anything else to my plate. Honestly, I've never really liked science, but if you ever need help with the soccer team, or anything in the music department or an upcoming play, then I'm your girl. That's the sort of stuff I love spending my time on.*"

There it is again, your co-pilot, doing a little butt dance and waving its hands over its head celebrating. You can hear the Bruno Mars music bumping in your head as your co-pilot does hip thrusts and gyrations celebrating you living YOUR life. You aren't being rude, dishonest, or confrontational. You are saying no to her, but so much more importantly you are saying yes to you. Yes, to the way you want to spend your time. Even better than that, you will be there and enjoying yourself when you help with a sport you love or with music and the arts!

Let the mom or dad who loves science be there for the science fair.

If Alice, or any other parent has an issue with it that's their trash to deal with. It isn't going to get caught on your grate and gunk up your life. You aren't going to give two thoughts as to whether or not someone has an issue with what you do with your time.

How many events with friends, phone calls, work emails, presentations, meetings, and moments do you take part in because you feel like you should, that it is expected of you, that it's the right thing to do?

Is there any value being placed on you and your time? How important is each call, each email, each event, etc., etc., etc.? Do you always let everyone else's needs come before yours?

Do you ever get to be first?

At what point do you allow yourself, and even better, give yourself permission to see value in your time?

To not be captive to what others assume you should do, what others expect you to handle, and what societal roles you are supposed to waste your time on.

In any given day, week, or month how much of your time do you spend doing things that aren't of your choosing? Twenty-four percent of your time? Sixty-three percent of your time? Eighty-seven percent? Ninety-six percent or even more?

Do you feel the drain of everything that doesn't honor who you are? Are there not enough minutes left in the day for you to do what you care about after catering to everyone and everything else?

Is that living your life?

When you pull out your phone to make a call and notice that the battery is running low, what is one of the first things you do? You go through and get rid of all the apps and stuff running in the background. You swipe away all the things that are draining the energy and sapping the battery from behind the scenes.

In life, we forget about all the stuff we have going on behind the scenes. All the things that at some point we said yes to, that are still draining our battery. The project you said you would help your co-worker out with. The friend who always leaves you exhausted after you hang out. The group you volunteered for. The committee you have to meet with once a month. The activities you do but don't care about. Pay attention to all those things, people, and events that you have said yes to that aren't needed. Clear them out. Get rid of them. Save the battery and your energy for you. Swipe them away.

Saying no to other people and other things helps us find time to do what we care about and put the real focus back on who we are and how valuable our time is.

That is the beauty of finding what you love and what fills you up. If everyone does that, there will be more than enough happy people helping in the areas that they are passionate about. The parent who loves science knows that volunteering for the fair is something he would enjoy spending his time on. It will fill him up, bring him joy and fulfillment and leave you with the freedom to spend your time on what you care about.

Where things fall apart and makes everyone miserable and pissed off is when we are constantly feeling obligated to say yes and then are left dealing with the results of saying no to ourselves.

Say yes to you. Yes, to your time.

Yes, to what you care about.

Yes, to life.

No to wasting your time. No to wasting your energy. No to wasting your life.

There is a huge difference between being selfish and self-honoring.

The Blue Goat chooses to put itself first, because if it doesn't no one else will.

17 DOMINOS

There is nothing more mesmerizing than seeing someone touch one black domino at the end of the line then watching as it quickly hits the next one and the next one, toppling them over one after another, weaving in circles and patterns.

Our life is much like a series of dominos. The momentum of our decisions and actions, over time, can make it where we can't stop them from getting away from us. Or we can be strategic and place the dominos one by one and control the fall.

We tend to think that the big stuff is all that matters. Who we marry, what job we take, where we go to college.

Yeah, they do matter. But it's so much more than that.

Our lives are made up of millions of little dominos that stretch for miles. When standing on a platform above them you can see all the different ways they can fall and all the different variations of ways things could go. All too often, though, we don't realize that all those choices and decisions we are given are each a single domino in the trajectory of our life.

Time and time, I hear comments like "*Court, I just don't know how I got here.*" "*Looking back, I can finally see why we ended up getting a divorce.*" "*This just isn't what I pictured for my career.*"

Over time you begin to realize how many choices you are making on literally a moment-by- moment basis.

You are faced with countless decisions and each one of those is a domino. Far too often we make choices that aren't in line with what we say matters most to us. We don't listen to our co-pilot and thus allow the dominos of our life to quickly get away from us and start a chain of events that can be hard to control or stop.

Do we thoughtfully hold each domino in our hand and pay attention to where it is being placed and know the direction we want it to fall? Do we simply put our lives on a certain "path" and follow the steps that the other sheep have taken and just let the dominos fall without paying attention?

You are deciding what college to attend. You are in love with one school, but both of your parents are alums from another college. Even though it is more expensive, they are happy to pay for you to go to their alma mater. You know how much it would mean to them; they've been dressing you in their school colors for as long as you can remember, and you know that you could get a similar degree and take over your parent's company in the future. Yet, you know that it isn't what you want. Do you allow them to choose that for you and start the dominos of your life moving in that direction? Do you let someone else determine the path that your life will unfold? Do you see or feel why you should be choosing another direction or a different path? Can you turn the domino to move the trajectory of your life into a direction of your choosing, or do you simply let someone else grab the domino and knock it over for you?

You continue to neglect your health, don't eat well and don't exercise. Year after year you know you should, but you just never do. Every moment that you make the choice not to make the change you know you should, you are continuing to knock over dominos that are taking your life down a path you know you don't want it to go. Sometimes the momentum of the dominos can get away from you and years of neglect can quickly lead to medical issues, the need for medication, or even a heart attack, because by continuing to do certain things you added momentum and didn't change the direction of the dominos and thus your life.

You wake up and eat a healthy breakfast and lunch but then have buffalo wings and beer for dinner. The dominos of your life were making small turns for the first few hours of the day, but then at dinner the direction was turned right back to where all the previous dominos have been headed for weeks and months before. Thus, no change.

You walk away from a promotion because you know in your heart that even though you will be making more money you will be traveling all the time and won't be able to see your kids. You decide that the extra money isn't worth what you would be giving up. Your dominos continue to fall in your chosen direction because the decision is based on honoring you and what matters most in your life. At that moment, you avoided the chance for the dominos to turn and start down an entirely new path heading in possibly the wrong direction.

Less time at home and the changes to your relationship with your kids, your health issues due to more work stress and less time to exercise, and the marital struggles from so much time apart were all avoided because of the choice you made.

Where are your dominos going? Were there opportunities in the past where you could have zigged, but zagged? If you could look at all the dominoes from high above, are your dominos close together and continuing to knock one another over heading in the wrong direction?

Or do you look down and see that you hold the next domino in your hand. When you look more closely, each one of your dominos is spread out far enough that if you pull one out, they all stop. Each domino is a decision that you make, knowing how important it is. You know you don't want to let the dominos fall without having control over them, or let others knock them over for you.

You pay attention to the decisions, no matter how small, and make sure each domino counts. You want each choice you make in life to not only matter, but to be about your life, nothing else.

You look at what angle and direction the domino will fall and what that might mean for the next domino. You place it on the ground and still take a more detailed look from above to make sure that this is the direction you want to head. Even more, you may take the time to consider where the next domino will fall too.

You are taking the time and analyzing and considering the impact of each of your actions. Slightly adjusting and twisting each domino to make sure it is going to fall where you want. You realize that each decision you make is going to take you closer to who you are and thus who you are capable of being, or further away from that person you want to become. You adjust the angle and make sure it is going to fall just right to continue taking the path you want.

It's important to remember, you might not be able to change where you are right away, but you can change the direction of where you are headed.

It's all based on taking the time to realize that your decisions, whether big or small, all have an impact on the outcome of your life.

Are you holding the next domino or is someone else? Are you paying attention to what direction it points?

Is it facing in a way that will take you down the path you want? When you are standing there looking at your life, do your friends come in and smack over the next few dominos and make numerous decisions on your behalf? Do you end up drinking when you didn't want to, hanging out with people you don't want to be with, sending your kids to a certain school, all because someone else chose? Do you look down and see three, four, five dominos that they already knocked over? Are there more? Have they put you in such a place that you are headed in an entirely new direction and the dominos are running away from you? Can you stop them from falling?

There are so many ways in life that others come into our world and make decisions for us.

Sometimes we should try and stop them from falling. Even tougher is taking it a step further. You might have to backtrack, turn around and put the dominos back up and start again. You racked up a bunch of credit card debt trying to keep up with your friends or take care of your family. You might have to tighten your budget, or make other major changes to fix bad mistakes you made in the past.

We can't be afraid of putting the dominos of our life back together and getting them exactly where we want them to be.

It may slow things down, but continuing to head in the wrong direction is far worse.

Each domino is taking you somewhere.

The dominos of your life are big versions of the little ones that you use to play the game on the table. They come up past your waist when you stand next to them. They are so wide that you can barely fit your hand around one. When you get up to the next domino of your life, put your hand on the top of it and take a moment. Think about all the options you truly have. That you aren't limited by anything other than what you want to create. There are no barriers to what is possible, what you are capable of, or what direction it can go.

Make each decision in your life so you have such passion and conviction about your actions that you hold the domino and then slam it down on the ground, knowing that what you are doing is your choice. BAM!!!

You know the decision is yours and exactly what you want to do with your life. The choice you made isn't a "*I hope this works out*" decision. It's an "*I'm me, 100%, and this is what I want with my life.*"

The domino hits the ground. You walk up to the next one, survey it and make sure it is angled just how you want it. BAM!!! Another decision that is who you are. BAM!!! You slam another one down with conviction. BAM!!! Another. Decision after decision with confidence, BAM!!! You walk up to each moment in life, each opportunity, BAM!!! You think about what it means, and what impact each choice will have on your life, next decision…BAM!! You slam it on the ground.

"I'm doing it!! I'm living!! Get the hell out of my way world!!!"

You are owning your life, crushing each decision and pushing out of the way anyone that gets near the decisions of your life. BAM!!! No one touches your dominos. No one makes decisions on your behalf, and no one determines what your life is going to look like.

BAM!!!

18 MAIN ATTRACTION

The coming attractions with the previews wrap up. The video with the larger-than-life versions of the Twizzlers and Whoppers, Diet Coke, and buttery popcorn finishes and the screen goes black.

The opening music starts as the theater lights go dark.

You grab a huge handful of popcorn, wiggle your butt to get comfortable and watch the opening title with excited anticipation.

The movie starts.

Maybe it is a touching romance, maybe a movie with amazing special effects, or an unexpected plot twist. Did it have fantastic cinematography or was it a hilarious comedy?

Movies are amazing because they work as a perfect representation of life.

There are movies that everyone knows and everyone talks about. Ones that are so memorable they have touched millions and ones that don't even make it to the theater.

Your life is a movie.

Right now, it is being made. The film crew is out on assignment filming and getting all the raw footage. The eighteen-wheeler is following you around everywhere you go with all the equipment. The sound guy with the big microphone on the end of a stick is running around behind you and the footage never stops.

At a certain point, the filming will be done.

When it is finally put together will it be a movie you want to watch? What will it make you think and feel? Is it inspirational; is there great depth and true passion and love? Is it going to be the type of movie that when it ends the audience is so overcome with emotion and the impact of what they've just seen that they sit in silence and try to take it all in? Do they have tears in their eyes because of how touching it was, or do they pop up out of their seat cheering and feeling the pure joy of what they just experienced?

Is your movie the one where as soon as "The End" pops up on the screen and the lights come on, people in the theater shrug their shoulders and say "*Meh. We should have waited until it came out on the DVR.*"

Do you live so that you can inspire people to think about themselves and their lives differently? Do others look at challenges in a new way because of what you did, how you lived and your inspirational perspective? Do you forget that you are that person? The one that has gifts that no one else has, which means you have the potential to live a life that has never been seen before?

You have the amazing opportunity to make a movie that only you can make. Much like the most talented producers, writers, actors and editors, you can surround yourself with the absolute best supporting cast possible.

If you aren't careful, you can quickly allow who you are and your story be drowned out by so many other things. The stuff that truly isn't the story. It doesn't tell who you are and doesn't share your gifts and put them on full display. You can allow the special effects, lighting and props to be a huge distraction, or even be the main things people pay attention to. You can be an afterthought if you aren't careful. Are you more worried about what is in the movie, rather than who your lead character is? Do you spend all your time reshooting and reshooting to get the right shot and are you using filters to make you look a certain way, or do you show the audience the rawness of who you are and let them get to know the real you?

Are they going to fall in love with a character who is like so many others they have already seen before, or someone they've never seen who has a new and genuine story to tell?

There has never been a perfect movie. Most importantly, producers know that they can't make a "perfect" movie. There is no such thing. You can't either. It's not a possible outcome, so rather than focusing on perfection, focus on the details. The plot, the music, the relationships, the joy, the heartbreak, and all the other aspects of your film that will make it stand on its own for the astonishing story it tells.

People want to see a movie that is real. Most importantly, there can only be one movie made about you. It is the most important movie, because there can never be another one made. There is no chance for a sequel. Make your movie one you would want to watch over and over again. One that every time you watch it you feel emotion, joy, sadness and laughter. You feel the rawness of a life lived. The full spectrum of life and all that comes with it.

What footage do you have so far?

Is it going to tell the story you want? Is the movie going to be one that inspires you, or one you wish you didn't waste your money on?

The script is still being written. The footage is still being filmed.

Where is your movie going to go from here? Is it going to end with a thud? Is it headed straight for the DVR section, or is it going to be a blockbuster?

There is no dress rehearsal for your life.

You get one shot at making this movie.

If it sucks so far be your toughest critic. Be honest. If the location isn't working and doesn't match the plot, move. If the other actors aren't doing their role, get a new supporting cast. If it is a boring movie, look to see how to bring energy and passion by focusing on the things that excite the lead character. Throw out the script. Re-write everything down to the last detail. The end result of what you are making is too important not to be willing to change everything.

No one wants to watch a movie about a sheep in the herd. There is nothing to see. People want to see what is going to happen to the Blue Goat as it explores the world, goes through challenges, and faces new experiences that no one else has ever seen before.

It's never too late to make a change. Some of the best movies are those that have a great plot twist or a surprise ending.

Maybe that is exactly what you need.

19 SOLO

You hear the alarm going off on your phone and you reach over to turn it off.

You wake up to find yourself in your bed just like every other morning. You walk down the hall, turn on the coffee machine and as your eyes start to wake up you look outside and notice something.

The view has totally changed. Where are you?

Before you are graceful streams and flower-crested hills with breathtaking mountains as far as the eye can see. The morning sun is just starting to flash its brilliance over the distant hills. You go back inside and shake your spouse and tell them something crazy has happened.

"You gotta see this! Come on!!"

You drag them out of bed in their groggy state and rush back to the kitchen, pulling as they struggle to put on a bathrobe.

You grab your cup of coffee and step barefoot onto the wood beams of the front porch. As your eyes continue to adjust to the morning light, you look around the left of the home and you can't see anyone or anything for miles. You hurry over to the other side of the porch and still nothing, just your home. The street you had lived on, the other homes, the mailboxes, your neighbors' cars, everything, gone.

"*What the hell happened??*" they ask.

"*I have no idea. What is going on? Where are we?*" you respond.

You go in and quickly change into jeans and a t-shirt to go out and try to figure out what is going on. Your car is there, but the paved street is gone, so you take off over the tall grass looking for answers.

Nothing.

When you get home, you search the house. Everything you had before is there with you. Your entire wardrobe down to each pair of socks you own. Your closet is still full of all the clothes that were there the night before. Every shirt, dress, and pair of pants, nothing is missing. Your entire entertainment center, your phone, wireless speakers and laptop are all still there.

Except it's just you two. The outside world is gone.

Day after day as you continue to search and explore, you find nothing but more fields, valleys of flowers, and snow-crested mountains. After spending more time exploring over the coming days, weeks and months, you realize you are truly all alone.

Over time you notice something starts to change. You begin interacting differently with the world.

You've finally started to wear your hair the way you always wanted to, but never did. Your dye-job is slowly growing out and you can finally see your natural hair color.

Your spouse started running because before they were always worried about how they looked on the treadmill and felt goofy running. They are feeling better now and are smiling more and have better energy.

You find yourself wearing the same few t-shirts that are your favorites. The music that you play is louder. You find yourself singing more than ever before. As the sun is setting, your spouse's favorite song comes on and you start dancing with reckless abandon. They start singing and you start to dance and shake your arms and bob your head to the beat as you let the music take over.

You realize that for the first time you aren't worried about anyone or anything else.

You aren't worried about what you do because for the first time in your life you aren't afraid of what someone else would say if they saw the real you.

You don't care about looking a certain way or what anyone else thinks because no one else is there to judge your decisions. You aren't concerned about being the person you think the world expects you to be, or some persona that others assume you are.

You get to be you.

The years come and go.

You realize that there has never been one conversation about getting a bigger home or moving. You haven't updated the kitchen, the bathroom, or anything else in the home. Everything works just fine the way it is.

You haven't taken a picture of yourself or your meal, because no one is going to see it. Instead you spend your time relaxing on the porch and talking.

You have the same car and yet there hasn't been any interest in getting a new one. Your spouse asks, "*Didn't you want to get a new car a while back before we ended up here?*" You respond, "*I did, but now I don't really see why we would.*" You still drive around plenty, but for some reason you don't feel the need to get a new car.

Over the years, the only things you needed were groceries, toiletries, and new shoes because of all the running. Luckily, Amazon has drones that allow you to order things and they still deliver. Yet, that is all you buy.

You notice that you haven't spent one second on what the latest fashion trend is or what other people are wearing. You just do and wear and live in a way that feels right for you.

Even though the drones can still deliver anything you want to buy, you aren't upgrading to a newer watch, getting different sunglasses for the summer, or a bigger TV during the holidays.

Instead, you find yourself immersed in the time you have with the person you love most and interacting with the natural world around you.

Why does it change so much?

If you were all alone and no one else could see what you do or what you buy would you still do and buy the same things?

Would you finally allow yourself to relax and enjoy what you have rather than worry about what you don't?

Is what you have finally enough?

Today, what is the thing or item that you still need? What is the moment or experience that hasn't happened yet? Is it a newer version of the computer you have, or the latest pair of exclusive shoes? Is it a prettier or more fit you? What is the thing that is missing?

When will you get that next item to put you over the edge, get you to the top, allow your cup to finally run over so you say, "*I don't need anything else*".

Is there ever going to be that moment in your life when you say "*I have everything I need*"?

Are we hamsters on a wheel? Are we constantly running and running for that next thing and then when we get there, we just think about what is *next* next thing? When can we can finally step off the hamster wheel and enjoy what is? Even when our cup runs over do we always look at the glass as half empty?

When we finally do get the new car, do we truly enjoy it, or do we soon find ourselves looking at the latest model with the newer body style and try to figure out how soon we can get it?

When is it all enough? Do we ever get to the finish line where we have enough things and stuff and look a certain way?

If no one else could see your new car, would you still get it? If you couldn't drive it to work and park it for others to see, or show your friends, would you be okay with what you have already?

Would you spend as much time on looking a certain way? Would you want to make sure you had as much stuff?

If all the purchases and things you bought weren't going to be seen by anyone other than you, would that affect what you buy?

If no one else would know where you went and what you did with your time, what would change?

How much of what we do and what we buy is predicated on what we think others will see, think, feel, assume, or say about us?

How much time, energy, money, and worry do we put into what others think about what we do or don't have? What would change if all your purchases and choices were being made without anyone else getting to see them or hear about them? Would you do the same things?

Would it allow us to spend less money on stuff we really don't need?

Would that give us so much more? Would it give us more time, more freedom, and less worry? Would we be okay with the house we have rather than worried about making it bigger, newer, nicer, and fancier? If our car does everything it is supposed to do, get us from point A to point B, do we need to worry about getting a newer version or bigger model?

How many of the choices we make create a life that is so much tougher than it needs to be? The bigger home, nicer wardrobe, newer car, huge shoe collection, countless pieces of technology all require us to make more and more money.

It means we need to work more, make more, get more, to keep up with a life we think we are supposed to be living.

If what you had was already enough, what would change?

Would you have to chase the next job that makes more money, or could you stay in the same role that allows you more time at home during the week and less time on the road? What would that do for your relationship with your family? What would change for you?

Do you have the courage and strength to keep the older car, not upgrade your home, not always have the newest everything moving forward? Is it possible that you can release all those things to put the power back in your hands? Is it worth giving up those things or better to not rock the boat?

We forget that we create almost all our stress by the financial decisions we make and we become bound to a life of being owned by our stuff. Our homes, cars, vacations, clothes: they own us. All those things hold us captive by keeping us from having the freedom to live the life we want. Without all the stuff, we would have more freedom, more flexibility, less stress, and most importantly more time.

What if you already have all the stuff and things but no real life of your own?

So many people I talk to say they feel like they are "Stuffocating". All the things they have are weighing them down, owning them, and can literally make them feel like they are suffocating under the weight of the life they are trying to keep up with. They have the initial desire to provide for their family, but then go right past that into thinking that there is then the need to do more and more and more for themselves and their children. They assume their spouse wants more, that the kids want more, and that they need more, but it isn't always the case.

This leads to less time together, often more pressure, and less happiness.

Then what do our choices say about how we value ourselves? Can we stand alone without the watch, bag, car, and other stuff? Without those items, is our life of any less value? Are we of less value?

If you do look at the decisions you make, are they honoring you and your life, or something or somebody else?

Are you worried about keeping up with everyone else in the herd, or, about being you?

Do the other sheep truly care that much about what you do or don't have, or is that something that you create in your head? How much time do you put into worrying about whether someone else has a certain outfit, car, or home?

As a result, we all too often spend money we don't have, on things we don't need, to impress people who don't care.

We get things and add props to our movie that don't add any real value, and in many cases, detract from what the main attraction really should be, you.

All the stuff forces us into a financial position where we have to work more, give more time, lose more sleep, have more stress, and be more frustrated to support these decisions we made that add no real value to our lives.

Can you live your life and make decisions based on what you want and how you want to live?

Are you too worried about not having the newest phone, most modern kitchen, and newest model of car? About people seeing what color your hair really is?

Are you letting the fear of what others may or may not think drive your decisions, or are you able to step out of the mess, into the clearing, and see that you have all the power to make decisions based on exactly how you want to live?

Can you dance and sing when no one is around? More importantly, can you do those same things and feel as great when they are watching?

Can you drive your car that isn't the latest model and say, "*YES, this is MY car!*" If anyone thinks less of you, let that crap go right into the sewer with the rest of the trash.

Can you see that someone caring about the model of your car says so much more about them than it does about you?

Is it possible that without those things you might even be a better version of you? Less weighed down, less stressed, and fewer things that take away from your life?

Can we break the chain of doing things based on what we think the world around us expects, or based on how we want to be seen?

Wake up into a new world of possibility. Act and live like it is just you. The magic happens when we realize that all the rest of the stuff doesn't matter.

Find the uncontrollable power in being seen for you, not some idealized version of you. Not someone surrounded and hidden by stuff and things.

If you want people to see you as an amazing person, simply be an amazing person.

20 VISIT IN THE NIGHT

Do you remember the day you were so mean to that kid in your Ancient History class in 8th grade, or cheated on your Calculus test? Maybe it was stealing something from the store in the mall or even just telling your parents a lie about where you were on a Friday night. There could have been bigger moments where you faked a report to make your company earnings look better than they were. Maybe you were a total ass to a complete stranger or snapped at one of your kids for no reason.

What was driving those emotions and decisions? Were you making choices that you didn't want to? Did you do those things to fit in, avoid confrontation, because you didn't feel good about yourself or you wanted to make more money? How do you feel about those things? Do you look back at those moments in your life and say, "*Yep, that is exactly who I am*"?

Or do you see a different version of yourself that you maybe aren't very proud of or even want to forget? What would you want to say to yourself just before that decision you made, that lie you told, or that business report you faked?

Right now, today, what decisions, choices, actions and emotions are you having that you will look back on the same way?

Are you repeating the past? Has anything changed other than the month and the year? Are you waiting for the "right time" to start doing the things you should do and acting like the person you want to be?

Are you waiting to become a father before you start living like the man a child would want to emulate?

Are you waiting to get to a certain age before you "grow up"?

Are you waiting for the New Year to finally start taking care of yourself?

We too often forget how truly powerful we really are. Not just in our own lives, but how the decisions we make can create ripples of change in the world around us. In the lives of people we care about and even those we may never meet.

What types of ripples are you sending out into the world? Ones that would make you say, "*Yes! That is me. I'm responsible for what I just did or what happened and how you are feeling,*" or "*Crap, I hope no one finds out that I was the one that did or said that.*"

It is amazing how doing what you know will honor your life is so different than that which dilutes the fabric of who you are and doesn't represent who you think you can be.

Unlike most nights when you go to sleep, tonight is going to be different. Later, you will wake up to see your younger self and the you that you might become.

Even knowing it is coming and anticipating the visit, you finally fall fast asleep.

You wake up to someone poking you in the shoulder and laughing. Your younger self has their face just inches away from your nose. "*Come on, stupid! Wake up!!*" They grab your shoulders and shake you as they laugh and mess up your hair. You struggle to figure out what is going on. You click on the light next to your bed and can finally see them.

You feel like you are looking in the mirror. "*Holy crap, it's me! I remember wearing that shirt! And those shoes, those were the coolest, I totally forgot I even had them!!*" You can remember exactly what it was like to be that younger version of yourself.

They sit you down and start to show you some of the old footage from your life. They turn down the lights and the tape starts to roll.

The movie starts to play and you remember so many great times as you watch moments that make you smile with joy and pride. The fun you had that day at the park for your birthday and the hilarious time you tried to make cookies. Running for class president in middle school. You totally forgot about that person who sat in front of you in class, who you had such a crush on.

Then they start to show you all the moments and decisions, choices you've made and what you've done that wasn't you. The lies, the deception, the rudeness, the attitude, all the stuff that you did that you just don't want to watch. The way you treated strangers, how big of an ass you were to your parents, how thoughtless you were to your friends.

You feel sick to your stomach. It's like you are watching someone you don't even know. There are moments where you know you are about to make a really mean comment to your sister and you are watching, thinking, "*What was I doing?*" You want to go back and stop yourself. You know you can't. The film footage finally gets caught up to yesterday and shows you getting ready for bed in the evening.

You look around and the younger version of yourself is gone. On the couch, you see your old favorite shirt. You pick it up and hold it for a second. You start to realize all the things that you've done and all the choices you've made. So many great memories, yet so many you wish you could go back and change.

It all went by so fast.

You didn't realize what some of those decisions would lead to and the impact so many of them would have for you and others.

You then feel a heavy hand on your shoulder. You turn to see yourself. Only this time you are much older. You look into your eyes and you don't see yourself looking back. You stare deeper and realize that you don't see anything behind the eyes. Your older self doesn't have any strength or vitality in its presence. You can feel the lack of energy. They look tired and carry themselves like a shadow.

Behind them appears another version of you. They too are older, but in a very different way.

Their posture is different. The second one stands up straighter; their spirit feels lighter. When your eyes catch, you can feel their energy. You can feel the power of who they are. Their look captivates you. They are vibrant. While they are both the same age, the second one feels almost youthful in their demeanor.

You ask, "*Who are you two?*"

"*We are your future,*" they respond in unison.

"*Well, which one is my future?*"

"*You tell us,*" they reply.

You can't change what you've done and what decisions you've made in the past.

Look deeply at the version of you you are becoming and decide which one it will be.

The choices you make and the actions you take will dictate how the movie will play out. Will the rest of the film be filled with more moments you wish you could take back, or moments that capture not only who you are but the version you want to become?

Will the choices you make lead to the version of you that is only a shell of the person you could have been?

Will you look back on all the filming of your life and have more and more cringeworthy decisions? How many more moments will you have that you wish you could take back and change when it is too late?

How often are you going to live in a way where you act like a jerk and you look to the cameraman and say, "*Oh no, please tell me you weren't filming that!*"

Or are you going to live a life where there are so many moments where you turn and say, "*PLEASE, tell me you GOT THAT ON FILM!!*"

Are you going to live today knowing that one day you will be that older version? You can decide moment by moment which one you want to be—if you want to be that present, energized, alive version or the one that lost their way so long ago that you barely recognize them.

The filming is going on. Look back and remember what you have done but more importantly think about what is yet to come. What version of you can you be? What version is the real you?

When your movie is over and the film is done, you can't go back and start over. You will either become a Blue Goat, or a sheep in the herd.

Moment by moment and choice by choice you are getting closer to, or further away from, each of the two future versions of yourself.

21 THERE IS A WAY OUT?

Plato's Allegory of the Cave is one of the most profound philosophical concepts in history. Plato describes how a group of people are chained in a cave and face a wall. Behind them is a fire, and they spend all their time watching the shapes and shadows on the wall that are projected from the light of the fire coming from behind them. What is projected on the wall in front of them becomes the prisoners' reality. They have no desire to leave for they know no better life.

Day after day they simply watch the shadows projected on the wall and think that the images they are seeing are reality.

One day they break their chains and finally realize that their reality is not what was being projected on the cave and not at all what they thought it was. They discover that there is not only a way out of the cave, but an entire life that they didn't know existed.

The contemporary world has seduced so many of us into being captives in the cave.

We are bound to a fake reality where the sights, sounds and expectations we pay attention to are only those we are intended to see. We are bombarded with minute-by-minute messages that dictate the reality that makes up the cave. Internet posts, news coverage, magazine articles, and advertisements are all the projections on the wall of the cave that we can't take our eyes off.

We are wrapped up in the latest fad, the hottest trend, the biggest celebrity gossip, political madness, the newest show and so on and so on. It never ends. It can't. Companies have to sell you stuff. Shows need to be watched so advertisers can make money. Magazines have to get you to buy them so they flash the biggest gossip story week after week. There is a continual bombardment of information, ideas, thoughts, stories, brands, and expectations.

The result is a life where all our focus is on what is in front of us rather than what is within us. Almost none of what we see, do, watch and read is about us. None of it is ours. Not an article, post, or story, or episode pertains to our movie. If you take a moment and turn away, do you realize that none of it is about you? We spend more time watching shows about someone else's reality than we do being present and living in our own.

Nothing is based on what you told anyone you cared about, are passionate about, or want to experience. Instead you are overwhelmed with the never-ending loop of information to keep you distracted.

What do you want?

What do you care about?

You can break from the chains and come to a new understanding of everything that is being shown on the wall and how much of your life it takes up. We forget just how little of our day is spent on our own interests.

We wake up and before we can even get out of bed we check our news feed or start to look at others' pictures.

As soon as we get in the kitchen or have breakfast we start watching TV and listening to the news and all the advertisements and stories about what we should be doing with our lives. In the car we listen to talk radio or the morning shows. At the red light we pull out our phone to see what is going on. All day at work you deal with the countless issues going on, constant emails, phone calls, proposal deadlines, marketing strategies, meetings, and you steal moments to check your news feed. You have no time for yourself.

When you do have a spare moment in the elevator, or waiting for your lunch order, you are back on your phone checking out the news, reading the celebrity gossip or checking your news feed again. You finally get home and then start to relax from it all and watch TV. Even during the commercials, we pull our phones back out to see what else is happening. Before lying down, you check again to see what is going on and what you've missed. You finally go to bed and then wake up and do it all over again.

We don't realize it, but we've created our own caves.

Do we ever wake up and take a moment to think about what we want out of our day, or do we immediately start looking at our screens to be told what is going on, what is important, and what to pay attention to before we even get out of bed?

Our TVs, phones, and computers have become the wall that the prisoners stared at all day and began to think was their reality. We take what we see, hear and read and that creates our reality. We forget that so many of the pictures have been photoshopped. The news covers stories in a certain way and we are being targeted for stuff companies think they can sell us. We are bombarded with so much information that at the end of each day how many thoughts of our own did we even get to have? Was there so much information being thrown at you that all you were doing was dealing with, deciphering and trying to make sense of it? Did you get a chance to consider what your own thoughts were? Or was everything based on reacting to incoming information?

Your thoughts, emotions, and insights are unlike anyone else's in the world. Yet we allow ourselves to turn off the amazing beauty of our own minds and let that be replaced with a scrolling feed on the wall in front of us.

We become captive to the feed and allow that to become the reality of what we do and how we interact with the world.

What if we turned it around? What if we turned it off? What if instead of checking the feed, listening to the news, or flipping through pictures, we just allowed our lives to create the entertainment? What would you find? What thoughts would you have if you gave yourself the time to let your inner voice and co-pilot talk? Is every moment of your day so planned and so busy that you literally don't have time to even think about what you want?

How many times have you gone to bed and then, suddenly, your brain starts going like crazy? You lie down and you have a million things to think about. For the first time all day, you finally turned off the flow of information onto the wall of the cave. The fire finally went out; the projection onto the wall stopped. For the first time, you gave yourself the chance to allow your thoughts to be heard rather than allowing everything around you and on the screen to be what you listened to.

"*Why can't I just relax and go to sleep. I need to get some rest!*" you think.

You are up half the night because you can't "turn it off" and get your thoughts to stop.

Now you add more stress, frustration, lack of sleep and maybe even medication to get some Z's because you can't slow down and turn your mind off. It's not because you are stressed out. It's because you never gave your own mind a shot at being heard until you put your head on the pillow.

Would you learn more about yourself if you turned away from the wall and looked the other way? If you spent your day actively participating in the moments rather than being constantly distracted by all of the noise and stuff going on in the world around you?

How much easier would it be to relax and sleep if all day you were aware of and listened to your own thoughts? If you did, when you finally decided to go to bed your mind would be tired too. You were listening, hearing and noticing what was going on and could handle your thoughts and emotions in the moments and let them pass.

You may realize that it doesn't take much effort to look behind you and see the real world.

If you pay attention, you can change your reality and how you see the world around you. Reality is not what is being projected and put in front of you. Reality isn't what we see on the screen. Yet we use the images that we are shown all day as the measuring stick by which we grade our lives. We see the million-dollar homes, the lavish lifestyle, bottles popping at the club, perfect bodies, smiling, well-behaved children, and amazing photo-worthy meals as the way to evaluate everything that happens and what we should be striving for.

We don't see the arguments, frustration, tears and hundreds of photos it took to finally get one where everyone in the family is actually smiling. We don't see all the cakes that were baked that fell apart before we see the one that finally looks perfect. We don't see how lonely the person is in the huge house with all the rooms that doesn't feel anything like a home.

We forget that most of it is fake. Created by others who think that is what things are "supposed" to look like. They too are doing what they think they need to be doing, to be the person they think they are supposed to be, trying to live the life they think they are supposed to be living.

It's not that the internet is bad; it's not that information in our hands and on our laptops is a terrible thing. It is all about how we access it and what we expose ourselves to.

Use those resources to explore and expand who you are. Watch videos that open your awareness and help you uncover your hidden gifts. Look for inspiration for the person you could be rather than being dragged down by what you aren't. If you aren't inspired, excited and confident after being online, then you should adjust the things and people you expose yourself to. If it isn't leading to positive thoughts and emotions, then you aren't being exposed to and following the right things. All the information, photos, videos and data can be great. We just should seek out the right mediums, the right speakers, the right people.

If you always feel bad after seeing what certain people post or say, it is time to filter out the negative information in your life. You will be amazed at the space it creates for something new.

Leave the crap, arguments, and mindless garbage for the sewer. You can always turn around in the cave and walk towards the exit. You can leave behind everything that is being forced upon you. Everything that you need and want to experience and discover is all around you and within you.

It's simply a matter of realizing that reality is not what is being projected in front of you. Life is not you being told who you are and what you need by what is on a screen.

What will you create with your life when you shift the focus away from everyone else and onto who you are and what you are capable of?

The sheep are constantly looking at the wall and wondering who is doing what, where someone is going, who has this or that. The Blue Goat doesn't care about what is going on with everyone else. It is too busy living its' reality than worrying about keeping up with someone else's.

22 WHAT DO YOU DO?

When we take a moment, and pause to look at all the other people in the world around us, what do we see? Are we interested in learning about who they are, what they care about and what makes them feel alive? Do we seek to learn from others and share our experiences to help and improve each other's lives, or do we simply see a measuring stick?

Are the people who live in our community, train in our gym, attend our school, and participate in our daily lives there to share and enjoy the most important aspects of life, or is it so much less than that?

How do we allow the people in our lives to matter and what do we want to find out about those we meet? Are we sincerely interested in other people's lives, or do we more often use our time together as a means to compare ourselves with others?

At the core, are we only interested in looking at them to see if they are better or worse off than us? Do we see strangers as a way to measure ourselves like standing on the scale to find our weight, or do we seek out to learn who they are? When we meet one another, how do we interact? What do we ask each other in order to learn something real and meaningful?

Our culture has made almost everything other than who we are to be the lens through which we determine the value and meaning of our lives.

Sizing each other up, comparing lives to one another, checking where we rank. We do it all the time. We often don't truly care who the people around us are. Instead, we care about where they are in life, whether they are ahead of us, next to us, or hopefully behind us in the herd.

When we meet, we don't ask each other questions that will lead to any real discussion or demonstrate any true desire to learn about the other person. Instead we choose to ask questions that provide us with information so we can make assumptions, assessments, and determine who we think the person is.

You get introduced to a stranger and the first question always is "*So…what do you do?*"

What are we really looking for?

You tell someone you are a teacher, and they immediately make assumptions about what type of person you are and how much money you earn. You tell them you are a CPA, attorney, salesman, or doctor and they immediately have an idea of what that means and who you are based on that career. Do we really think that we, and other people, are no more than cardboard cutouts of what each profession represents?

Do we slot so smoothly into the category of what it means to be an investment banker that people are right when they picture you as a jerk who doesn't care about anyone or anything beyond money and what it buys? Do we let stereotypes dictate not only how we see the world, but how we live in it? At what point do we find that we are so much more than what we do and what we have?

What we do is such a small part of who we are. Yet people use what you do and where you live as a means by which they can compare and justify their choices and feel better or worse about themselves.

If comparing and contrasting is the goal, then we are asking the right questions.

What if we want more, though? What if we determine that what we do and what we have isn't even remotely close to who we are.

Unless that is all there is.

When we spend years chasing the Golden Eggs, wasting our time on the yellow brick road and trying to conform, we can become attached to what we do and what we have. With nothing else real or meaningful in our lives, those things can become our identity.

We allow ourselves to be defined by where we live, what we drive, our alma matter, and what we do. The stuff and things around us becomes the fabric of who we are.

If we allow ourselves and our identity to become wrapped up, intertwined and one with what we do and have, then how do we possibly handle it when those things change?

Your entire life you've played football and were a star in high school and even throughout college. You have always been known as the football guy. The star athlete, the guy with all the trophies, awards, and accolades for what you did on the field. The last whistle has blown, the game is over and football ends. What now? If you don't have that anymore as part of who you are, who do people see? Who looks back when you look in the mirror? Are you the guy at the bar still talking about the big game from five years ago? If you aren't the football player anymore, who are you?

You were at a startup for four years and helped grow it into a real business. Everything about what you did was the "entrepreneur", the person who went out on her own and started something. You take a new job and now you are just another employee in a big company. How do you deal with not being the cool person in the small company that was changing the world?

You've always had the newest gadgets and toys. Everyone knows you as the guy who drives a Mercedes because that is all you have driven for the last ten years. After a job loss, you realize that you really can't afford one. Are you affected by not having that car? Do you feel different or worry you won't be seen as successful because you don't drive a Mercedes anymore? Are you going to go into debt or burn up savings just to make sure you still have that car?

Do the jobs, things and activities begin to make us up, or are they just small spices and seasoning in the life we create? If you take out the sports, the car, or the job, does that take away a huge part of who you feel you are?

When we interact with others, are we looking to find out more about who they are or simply looking to find out what stuff or things they have to see where we stand?

Do we ask questions that are more about us sizing people up than getting to know them?

"So where did you go to high school?"

"*Where do you live?*"

"*Where did you go this summer?*"

These aspects of our lives have become ways that we subtly check each other out, try to get a sense of where everyone else is in the herd.

After meeting a new person how many times are you thinking about all the amazing things you learned about them? You think "*Wow! That guy is amazing, how cool is it that he gets up and runs with his dog every morning and it sounds like he really loves working with his son's basketball team as the assistant coach!*"

More likely we are thinking, "*Holy crap, we are the same age and they already live in Beverlywood?!? He must be making at least six figures, and if his kids are going to Anderson Prep, he must be doing really well. I noticed his shoes and that suit looked expensive. I couldn't tell what brand his watch was, but it sure didn't look cheap! Yea, he seemed nice, but I bet he is a real jerk behind closed doors.*"

Deep down, we don't really care what others are passionate about, what others love, what makes people smile and feel alive. We are more worried about us. We are worried about falling behind or not stacking up.

How many times are we truly happy for others when they are successful? How often do we meet someone who is doing well and have positive thoughts about them and what is going great in their life? Do we immediately think about what we don't have, what isn't going well and how much luckier they are than we are? Or are we able to truly find joy in the success and happiness of those around us? Can you feel joy for the friend, for the stranger, or does his success drag you down because you don't have the same things?

When you meet someone, or interact with a friend, pay close attention to what you think and feel about him or her. Not what you say, but what you feel and think. Are you having positive, energetic, supportive emotions, or do you hear nothing but negative, judgmental, and critical thoughts? If that is how we are viewing others, what does that say about us? Why are we so quick to judge the people we meet and see?

Do we have negative thoughts about a stranger in the grocery store? You look at what they are wearing, how they look, how they carry themselves and immediately begin to judge, assume, and throw trash onto their grate for no reason.

We need to take that negative energy and throw our own trash into the sewer rather than on someone else's grate.

Is the goal to make real connections and uncover opportunities for new relationships, or to simply test out the competition and use what we do and what we have to express our status to the world?

Your job is not who you are. Your job or role is a small part of the much more important movie of your life. It is a small subplot that may change numerous times over the course of your life, but it still isn't who you are. You aren't where you live. Your gift to the world is not what car you drive or where you went to college. That is not who you are; those are just props and scenes in your movie.

Too many of us have let what we do or what we have represent who we are.

When you pass away, how much is going to be written about what your job was or where you lived? Is your legacy "Karl Anderson, Doctor, Range Rover, $775,000 Home, Ivy League School, Nice Clothes" and nothing else?

When you get to the end of the journey, your legacy is not what your job was or what you had. Your legacy was how you loved your family, how you made other people feel and what you did that changed the world around you.

Your life will be measured by how much you contributed, not how much you had.

Imagine if you asked someone:

"What do you love to do outside of work?"

"What is going great in your life?"

"What are your kids passionate about these days?"

"What is the best part about being a parent?"

The list can go on and on.

What would you learn or find out? What sort of connections and deeper conversations might you find?

What would happen if we gave up comparing? How would things change for us if we cheered on everyone else? What would we feel if we were excited about the success of others?

How different would your energy be if you never worried about comparing your life with the lives of others? How different would you feel if you focused on living your best life and were a huge fan for all those around you?

It's time to stop looking outward for comparison and to hold up the mirror to ourselves.

Figure out who that greatest version of yourself is and who you can be.

That is your measuring stick.

Chase that.

23 BUNGEE CORD AND ROPE

If you take a moment and listen to your thoughts, what do you hear? Where do your thoughts take you?

How much time have you spent just since you woke up thinking about something that happened a week ago, a month ago, a year ago? A breakup, the loss of a loved one, a mess at the office, a fight with your friend. How much time have you spent re-living a moment that has already come and gone? You're still pissed off about a text, the bad meeting, or you still feel anxiety about the big presentation that you totally blew.

What about all the stuff you have coming up; the big exam next Thursday, what to wear to the cocktail event this weekend, what gift to get for your friend's birthday party, if your son will be picked on again in class?

What to say to your friend when you finally see her since you've been thinking about telling her off for two weeks now? You've already had the conversation in your head over a hundred times.

"*I'm going to tell her how upset I was that she said that*," you think.

"*But if she says that shouldn't have upset me, oh MAN, I'M GOING TO GO OFF ON HER!!*"

You get all pumped up just thinking about the confrontation. How you are going to tell her off, what you are going to say. You can almost see the conversation unfolding. You picture it happening, you hear what you say and her response and what you say to that, back and forth. You go over and over the scenario in your head.

You finally see your friend for coffee. She sits down and after taking a slow sip, she says, "*I am so sorry for what I said last week. I've felt terrible about it since I saw you, and I just didn't know what to say. I hope we are okay.*" "*Well, crap*," you think. "*She really was sorry. She is the best; I suck for thinking she didn't care.*"

All the time, energy, stress and worry you put into that moment was wasted. Wasted on something that never happened. You lost all the time you could have been present doing other things.

As we wake up and start to experience each day, we are experiencing the amazing timeline of life. The moving walkway that never stops. We get on and whether we want it to or not, life keeps moving. Yet we are almost never in the here and now. Our mind and our thoughts are almost always on something that has already taken place or something that may or may not happen in the future. Why do we do this to ourselves? We pine over the pain, misfortunes, and issues of the past.

How often do you find yourself re-living your proudest moments? The big exam you studied all week for and got an A, the day you helped your child to learn how to ride their bike, the great round of golf with your father. Are those the past thoughts that you think about often? Or is it the moments that didn't go as planned, is it the pain, the frustration of what could have or might have been but wasn't?

We spend so much of our time thinking about the stuff from the past. Even worse is when we think only about the bad things.

We feel the moments of anger, frustration, and disappointment from our past pulling at us. We feel the constant need to rehash, rethink, and relive moments that do nothing but sap our energy and upset us.

Even though your body is here today, there is a bungee cord wrapped around your ankles that is trying to drag you back into the past. It doesn't want you here. It wants to pull you back to re-live, go over and stress about things and events that can't be changed. The love you didn't have from a parent. The job that ended terribly. The anger over being wronged by a friend. The hurtful words your brother said to you. The ex that cheated on you.

The memories are nothing but that. Moments in our lives that came and went. Yet we continue to make the past a part of our present.

Only you can't change anything.

The raw film footage is part of what happened in your life. Every moment is an incredible gift that helps tell your story. What happened in the past, whether amazing, or terrible and painful, isn't who you are. It is only a part of your story. It is a few moments or even a few years in the movie of your life. All too often we take a terrible time or sad event and think it is the entire movie, or we allow it to be a part of every scene.

Who are you punishing for continuing to hold on to those bad moments? The person that screwed you over? He would be laughing to know that you are still thinking about something that happened three years ago. The ex who broke your heart? She is already married with two kids and you are still thinking about the night she left. Who is that helping? Is your goal to make him or her feel something or hold them accountable? The only person still thinking about the moment is you. They have moved on.

As you've been reading this book are you able to enjoy this moment, or are you already thinking and worrying about what you have to do tomorrow? Are you constantly thinking about that meeting you have next week or a tough conversation you know you need to have with your parents?

Is the rope of the future and what is coming wrapped around your wrists? Are you constantly being pulled into a time that hasn't even happened yet?

How hard is it to be present when all you can think about or worry about is something that hasn't even taken place?

What would change if you let that go? What would change if you allowed yourself to cut the bungee cord that is pulling you into your past and the rope that is trying to pull you by the wrists into the future? How would that make you feel? Would you experience today differently? If all your energy and emotion was about what is happening right this very moment—the way the paper feels in your hands and the feelings and thoughts you get from reading this book. Do you give yourself permission to be in the present? The hardest part is that the present is constantly moving. Time is going to happen whether or not we want it to.

What does this kind of time pressure (from both ends) do to our body and our energy? If we have a bungee cord trying to drag us back into our past while a big rope is pulling us into the future, how does that make us feel in the present?

If so much of your energy is spent on giving in to the bungee cord and the rope, there will be nothing left for you today.

Can you embrace the fact that you don't have to worry about what you are going to make for dinner right this moment so you can enjoy reading *Blue Goat* for a while? Tomorrow, you might be able to relax and have fun at lunch with your friends rather than worrying about getting home and catching up on your work emails. How would your moments change if you were there for all of them? Not just present physically but present with your thoughts, attention and emotion.

The gift of the moment is not a new idea. Rather, the ability to be physically and mentally there for the moment may be. It's bad enough to miss events and moments that you look back and regret not being there for. Just as bad is looking back and realizing that you were there, but you were checking emails, texting someone, or worrying about something from a few days ago, or weeks away.

Fretting over what happened in the past will never change what took place.

Your worry today won't change the outcome of your life in the future. Yes, you need to plan—but planning isn't worrying. Planning is taking your available knowledge, considering options and making choices. You'll save this much money, do this much exercise, and act with passion, BAM! You make the decision, take the steps you need to take, and live in the moment. Planning is sensible. Lying awake all night worrying if you made the right plan isn't.

Your stress and worry today won't change whether something will or won't occur. You have limited ability to change how the moments and timeline will unfold. Some things are under your control and some aren't. What isn't under your control won't change by picking at it with your mind. What you can do, always, is enjoy the moments and realize that being present is truly one of the greatest gifts you can give yourself.

Being present and being one hundred percent in the space where you are living each moment will take you exactly where you need to be in life. If you do that each day, you will continue to go exactly where you need to be heading. Listening to your co-pilot and living your life will allow your days to unfold as they should.

In living with clear intention, your focus isn't on the future, because you are taking each moment and living it to make sure your present is exactly what it should be. As the days begin to unfold you will be living each moment knowing you are right where you need to be.

If each moment, choice, and day unfolds with you making decisions with intention, then whatever comes from your next moment and year will be exactly what is supposed to be for you. The movie of your life will start to write itself.

In our life, we too often only want to enjoy and live in the moments that are fun and enjoyable. Life isn't easy, there are going to be hard, possibly terrible moments. We can't run away from the pain of life. Too many of us try to hide from the hurt. If we stay present in the moments that aren't great, we can choose to live them and experience them when they happen. When we try not to deal with a loss, or a painful experience, we will be forced to carry that with us until we finally do live it. Thus, what was a terrible day or period in your life can last for so much longer. We end up letting that hard time or tough event be a part of every scene in our movie. Allow yourself to be in pain, feel the sadness, suffer the heartbreak. Allow yourself to live in those moments. Feel everything you need to feel by being present. Only then can you know that no matter how bad the moment was, you've lived and experienced it and moved on. If you don't, when the great moments do occur, they will be clouded and lessened by the pain or suffering you are still carrying with you.

I'll never forget the morning I was walking on the beach with my now wife the day of our wedding. We were up with the sunrise and went for a walk. My thoughts weren't about whether people would like the food, if it was going to rain or be too hot, if the music was going to get everyone dancing, if we would start a family soon, or if everyone was going to get along. I wasn't thinking about my past or our future. I was only focused on being there in that moment with her. I was there feeling the sand through my toes, smelling the crisp ocean air and thinking of nothing other than walking with her.

In that moment, I caught a look from her I will remember for the rest of my life. She turned and gave me a slight glance with a smile and right then the sun caught the corner of her eye, her hair blew in the wind, and she was the most radiant thing I had ever seen. It was truly like a moment out of a movie. Then I realized it was. My movie. I was there. I'll remember it until the day I die. Being present in that moment gave me one of the most treasured images of her I will ever have and I didn't miss it.

24 ONE DEGREE

The notion of making changes in our lives can feel overwhelming. Having to wake up earlier to work out or meditate can seem like it takes a herculean effort. Figuring out when and how we are going to simply go for a walk, or even just slow down and have time to cook a meal can feel impossible. Far too often, the excitement of change gets lost in the reality of what it takes. As a result, we go through days, weeks, and years of our lives doing the exact same thing.

How can we make real change in our lives without it taking so much effort, so much work and so much time? Is there a way that we can shift our view to realize just how much we are capable of? We want to do great things and be someone who leaves a mark on the world, but where do we even start? Is it possible that you are capable of such feats, or is your calling just to be an extra in everyone else's movie?

You can't for a moment think that you were made just to be another faceless sheep in the herd. Every life, every person, YOU, are an amazing gift that has a reason for being here. The issue is that we get complacent, comfortable and satisfied with the limited view of what is possible. How does that change? Is it possible to do it in small ways or does it require you to change your entire life overnight?

Let's say you place a pot on the stove with the goal of heating up water. As you turn the burner up to medium, the water will slowly get warmer. After a few minutes, you can't even stick your finger in the water for fear of getting burned. If you reach down and turn up the dial to high you can put your hand over the water and can feel it getting hotter and hotter. Using a thermometer, you can see the temperature continue to rise. Ninety-five degrees, a hundred, 143, 189, 211.

Then something amazing happens. For every degree the temperature was increasing, the water was just getting hotter and hotter. Then all of a sudden the temperature goes from 211 degrees to 212 degrees. Just like before, the water got hotter, but now something else has happened. That one extra degree, that one slight additional amount of heat, changed everything.

What was just a pot of water became a pot of hot water that is now boiling. The water is now creating steam. With the right apparatus, you could harness the power of this boiling water and use the steam for amazing outcomes. The steam that came from this one extra degree of change is strong enough to start and move an entire engine. It can power machines, boats, trains. It can move structures that are tens of thousands of pounds. These machines can move water and earth. This steam can be used to move mountains. One extra bit of heat caused the water to fundamentally change.

It might be a simple moment when you start to feel that one degree of change. Tomorrow, you finally say "Yes" to yourself rather than to something you don't want to do. Later this week you decide to run an extra five minutes on the treadmill or make a smoothie for breakfast. You start to make one degree changes in your life. These moments are slowly changing you. At first you might not be able to see what is happening but over time you will begin to change. Moment by moment, choice by choice you will start to change. The most important thing about getting water to boil is that the heat never stops increasing. Just like your life, you can't stop the quest for something better for yourself. It may not take everything you have, just one extra degree of effort every day. In time, you will slowly become the real you. The you that has more power than you ever thought possible. The you that is bursting with enough energy it can literally move mountains.

The degree of change will also directly impact where you end up on our journey. As you live, if you start moving in a direction that is one degree different than the rest of the herd, at first it may not seem like a big difference. Over the next few days and weeks you will start to notice that you are only a few hundred feet away from everyone else. The longer you keep choosing to head in the direction you believe is right for you, the more things will change. Your distance from the herd will grow. That one-degree change, over time, will mean you are thousands of miles away from the masses. Leaving you on a journey that is yours alone. From that small bit of extra effort, that one degree of becoming more yourself, you can change everything.

Blue Goats aren't afraid of change. They wrap themselves in courage for the journey ahead. They feel strength and excitement for the life that will unfold when the small changes add up to much larger ones.

Blue Goats know that sometimes it begins with the smallest change. It may be getting up to work out or simply calling your parents more often. The one degree of change is what starts everything. You have to decide where to start. The small changes are what add up to a life that is removed from the herd. One where before you were trudging over the mud with the rest of the sheep, you now find the power to change the world around you.

The temperature of the sheep is lukewarm bathwater.

The Blue Goat's water is bubbling with energy and thick steam in the air above.

Find that little bit, the inspiration, the energy, the love, whatever it takes. Find it.

That one extra degree.

Instead of just getting by at 211, become the you that lives at 212 degrees.

25 SNOWFLAKE

When you were born, you were unlike anyone that has ever come before and will ever come again.

The placement of every freckle and hair is different than anyone else's. The precise shade of your skin, the length of your arms and legs, the shape of your ears and eyes are yours alone. Your thoughts, the timbre of your voice and your emotions are distinct from those of any other child. From that beginning the intricate fabric of what it means to be you is woven.

In the days and weeks that follow, small expressions of who you are begin to be shared with the world. The way you smile and laugh, funny things you do with your hands when you wake up, the way you sleep, how your body moves when you breathe, and even how you smell.

You were unlike anyone else when you were born. Yet being born doesn't make your life immediately different from anyone else's. We want our lives to be great. We want to be that unique snowflake but it doesn't turn out that way. We so badly want people to see us and how we show up in the world and say, "*Wow, you are amazing and special!*" but they don't.

The reason why is that all too quickly we take those gifts, the personal thoughts, special qualities, emotions, passions, and intuitions we have and filter them to ensure that we only highlight those feelings, actions, and ways of living that fit into the mold of who we think we are supposed to be.

We go from being a snowflake that, when looked at under a microscope, has an exceptional patchwork of thousands of beautiful edges, points, delicate patterns, wonderful depth, and intricate design, to very quickly looking like the holiday version of a snowflake that you cut out of paper during Christmastime.

A child sitting in a classroom with a pair of scissors and a piece of white paper can quickly fold up the paper and with a few snips make a long chain of perfect snowflakes. Ones that all look alike. Snowflakes without any real detail or design and ones that are almost impossible to tell apart. There is nothing that makes one stand out from the next, nothing that makes any of them special. What should be a unique, individual snowflake is instead the same as countless others.

We think of ourselves as special. We expect the world and the people around us to move out of the way, get excited or be impressed by us for no other reason than because we are ourselves. There's a truth to that—we are special. Yet we don't get the feedback or results we expect and can't figure out why.

How do we go from being the real snowflake of infinite details and design to the cardboard cutout? When do we lose everything that makes us exceptional and instead allow ourselves to be okay with the cutout version that is being made by someone else's hand?

Without realizing it, we sacrifice the amazing gift of our one life and the opportunity to develop and express what is special about us. We throw away the chance to chart a new course, share our gifts, explore our thoughts and emotions.

What starts out as an opportunity to create a life unlike any other quickly gets replaced with the desire to conform, fit in, and be like everyone else. (Yet still be seen as special.) Instead of exploring the details of who we are and looking at our sharp and curved edges and seeing the amazing patterns and intricate shapes, we instead look to mold our original design into that of the other snowflakes as quickly as we can.

Therein lies an important question: What does it mean to be different?

What does it mean to be you?

How can you determine if your decisions are truly your own and based on your dreams and goals rather than based on external forces?

What does it mean to live YOUR life?

Who you are and the gift of your life is the opportunity for you to share those amazing edges, shapes, patterns, and details of who you are with the world.

When given the choice between a real snowflake and a cardboard cutout, people choose the real one every time. People want what is genuine. We want to look at things in more detail and discover what makes them amazing and different from all other things. Yet, when it comes to our lives, we instead choose to be the cardboard cutout and allow everything that is happening around us to keep us from being true to who we are.

Share you with the world. Don't hide all the beauty that you have and the amazing details and intricacies of who you are.

So many of us have heard that we are a snowflake. That we are one of a kind. That there is no one else like us. We get participation trophies and we get rewarded for doing nothing other than being present in life.

You aren't special just for showing up in life.

It's time to be an original, not just in some parts of your life—in every part of your life.

It's time to look inward. To take out the magnifying glass and really see who you are. Look for every piece of you that makes up your life.

You've always heard you were a snowflake.

It's time to finally decide if you are a cardboard cutout like so many others or the real thing.

26 BLUE GOAT LIFE

The World Needs You.

Every moment of every day you get to decide what that means.

Later today and tomorrow you are going to be faced with countless small and maybe even big choices and decisions. Each of those moments and decisions is helping to create your movie and make your future. Those choices can be based on listening to the co-pilot that is giving you direction for where you should be, or they can be based on all the noise coming from the world around you. Without a sense of who you are and what matters most, you are destined to make decisions that won't get you closer to the future that you want. You end up walking with the herd heading towards the red pin with everyone else.

It's time to be you.

When you start to listen, things will begin to change. When you choose to live based on what you want, based on what matters to you, and because you are working from a place of abundance rather than from a place of lack, you will start to have 'Blue Mist Moments'.

You know when a cartoon character has an amazing thought and a huge explosion bursts just over his head? You will begin to feel that. When you choose to go on your path, seek out your purpose, say yes to yourself, or ask "why" about life, you change everything. The Blue Goat that is you will have a burst of blue mist explode out of the top of your head. Your co-pilot will be shooting off a huge cannon of Blue Mist in the air. Like a whale shooting water out of its blow hole, every moment, choice and action that you take away from the herd and closer to you is a 'Blue Mist Moment'.

You should look and feel like you have blue mist exploding out of you at all times. A shower of choices and actions that are all yours, ones that keep you on your journey and your path. Your co-pilot will be having a party and a constant celebration from the choices you make and the cannons of blue mist they continue to shoot off. It will be dancing and partying to your favorite music, shooting off cannons and feeling the exhilaration of living your life!

Your days will be filled with 'Blue Mist Moments', just like being showered with confetti on stage after winning the big award.

Your life isn't there for you to have; it is something you must do. Life needs to be turned into "living". You can choose to live without any effort, or you can choose to put in effort and make it happen. Sometimes that effort is just one degree of small change, which over time will lead to the world around you changing. Just like you choosing to read this book, you can decide what you want to do with the priceless moments that you have left.

You can finally accept personal responsibility for not just having the right mindset but taking the right actions for yourself and your life. The life you want, not the one you are supposed to want.

Life is not static but rather an event taking place at every possible moment. Minute-by-minute basis you make choices to determine whether your "life" is one of your doing or not.

What you do or don't say yes to. Where you live. What job you take. Whether you are thoughtful to the stranger or throw trash on their grate.

Thus, your final movie will be the result of a million different decisions.

If you truly are the unique snowflake you are capable of being, then when your red pin drops, it will never be where anyone else's pin has been before.

We aren't all the same, so we aren't all supposed to have the same end result.

Life then, is not a matter of looking to achieve homogenous results but rather a scattering of outcomes and very different pictures. Yet, on a daily basis our choices and more importantly our actions are largely driven by a herd mentality. We work so hard to keep up with all of the other sheep and thus all end up at the same unfortunate outcome.

Do you know if the paved highway is going to not only get you where you want to go, but more importantly take you on the journey that will provide you with the experiences and life you want?

When you stay in the herd on the highway you will find that when your blue dot gets closer to the red pin, the cars will slow down. Like a huge traffic jam with nowhere to go, you find yourself bumper to bumper with the car in front of you. You've reached the end.

The countless cars ahead of you inch ahead and then slowly give up, and all begin to stop. You slowdown in the middle of the highway and pull up to the car in front of you. You look around and see brown sunburned fields. The landscape is barren. No grass, trees, or animals. No flowing streams or majestic mountains and flower-filled valleys.

Just the concrete paved highway, deserted dry fields and one large billboard in the distance.

Everyone is expecting the Emerald City and the deliciousness of the sweet chocolate from the final Golden Egg.

You shift your car into park. Looking around, you notice that everyone else is getting out of their cars. There is nowhere to go. No exit, turnoff, or place to make a U-turn. You've arrived at the end. All the cars ahead of you are stopped too, and you turn to see more cars pulling up right behind you. You turn off the car, grab your keys and slowly get out of the car. Nervously jangling the keys in your hand, you walk between the cars and see countless other people getting out of their cars, all walking towards a tall billboard to see what it says.

Navigating through the parked cars and the other people, you get closer and see that the billboard looks old. The color has faded, the corners are ripped, and you can see the wind causing torn pieces to flap against the wood frame in the breeze. There is a huge crowd gathering to look at it.

In its faded color the large billboard shows a party. It has men and women that look like they are dancing around a record player. A few of them hold cans that say "Beer" and others appear to be laughing and smiling as they smoke cigarettes. They are in dancing poses, partying and listening to music.

In letters that look like the Coca-Cola font it says: "*You made it!! Time to celebrate!!*"

In the background, you can faintly hear a familiar song crackling and going in and out over old speakers. You recognize the beat, but can't tell what song it is. As you slowly move closer, you lean in and you can finally start to hear it better. The song becomes clearer and you can finally make out the words.

"*Ceeeeeeee LE Bration time COME ON!! Da da da da da da da Yaaa Hooo!*

"*Ceeeeeeee LE Bration time COME ON!! Da da da da da da da da Yaaa Hooo!*

"*There's a party going on right here… A celebration to last throughout the years…so bring your good times, and your laughter too, we're gonna celebrate your party with you…Come on now!!*

"*Ceeeeeeee LE Bration. Let's all celebrate and have a good time!!*"

It's "Celebration" by Kool and the Gang.

You look around and everyone else that has gathered in the crowd looks just as confused as you are. You can hear people asking each other in hushed nervous tones, "*What is going on?*"

You remember Karl.

"*Wait….this is it???*

This is what we were all working our entire lives for?

There is nothing here!!!

There is an old dilapidated billboard of people smoking at a party and "Celebration" on the radio!

What the HELL!?!!?!"

You spin around to your left looking…searching for answers.

Nothing.

Just more empty cars and other people who are just as scared trying to figure out what the hell is going on.

You look around to your right and walk over to the concrete barrier and look out over the barren fields.

Still nothing.

Behind you, there are more cars coming. You can see miles and miles of cars coming to the same place, all starting to slow down as they get closer to the end.

You put your hands on your head. Everything feels like it is spinning around you. You start to shake in a state of complete shock.

You can't believe it.

You start to think, "*I've spent my entire life to get here. And this is it…*

"This… is the end?!?!?

You have got to be KIDDING ME!!!!

NOOOOOOOOO, NO, NO, NO, NO, NOOOOOO!!!!!!"

WHAT DID I DO?!?!?!?!"

You scream as you slam your hands down on the top of an empty black car next to you.

You drop your head down below your waist and your hands to the top of your knees as you start to feel faint. You can feel your heart racing and your chest rapidly moving trying to keep up with your frantic breath. Looking between your feet at the concrete, you try to control yourself. You feel like you are going to pass out as you struggle to slow down your breathing and relax.

You are shaking your head as you struggle to figure out what has happened. You have no idea where you've ended up.

Your breathing finally starts to slow down. You put your hand on the ground and half fall over against the tire of the black car and sit up against it. With your right leg extended, you hold your left leg against your chest and close your eyes.

All you can feel is your heartbeat and the gravel underneath you.

You take a deep breath in and holding back tears you slowly look up to the sky.

It all starts to come together and make sense.

You look back out over the scene.

It finally dawns on you what is really going on. The billboard is old because people have been trying to get to this same place for decades. You can see it now. It's on a big set of old worn-out wheels. They've moved the billboard closer, but behind it are millions of cars that obviously came here before you.

Millions of people that made the same trip, flying down the highway, passing one another trying to get to the same place. Only once they got here they realized it was too late to turn around.

They got to the end to realize they'd spent their entire life on the yellow brick road, trying to get to the Emerald City.

For years and years they worked as hard as possible with the promise of great things ahead. They gave up all their hopes and dreams with the expectation of amazing things to come and then after sacrificing so much, they made it to the end.

Everyone was racing through the days and years, and after everything they were finally shown the truth.

It was all a bunch of bullshit.

Millions of people on the same road trying to get to the end and the promise of something great. They just didn't know what the end was. No one asked, "*Why are we going where everyone else is going. What is actually at the end of the road?*"

Do they know it is just going to be a big old dilapidated billboard showing people having fun smoking cigarettes with Kool and the Gang playing in the background?

Why the hell would we want to come here!?!?

No one told us that there is nothing at the end of this road.

No one told us that everything we were racing to get to is an empty promise.

No one told us that we would give up everything and the one life we have for nothing.

I never stopped to think about where I wanted to go and what I wanted out of MY LIFE.

What events, moments, or scenarios will provide us with the inspiration to step onto the higher ground or the rocks around us and survey not only where we are, but more importantly where we are going and where we will end up?

What will have to happen for us to start paying attention?

Will it take a terrible diagnosis, a bad accident, or a near-death experience for you to finally wake up and realize that life is happening? Can you change before you are forced to change?

Will you take the time to zoom in on the map and see all the roads you can take and paths that are possible on the journey, or do you just look at the red pin that everyone is heading to and worry about getting there as fast as you can? Do you even know where the red pin is, or who put it there? Since the red pin is you living your last day do you even know when you will get there? Are you finally going to want to turn around when you are taking your last breaths and pulling up to the old billboard?

Will it be too late?

That opportunity is always still there, no matter how far on the journey you have traveled in the wrong direction. You might piss off some people around you and frustrate people who don't understand why you're driving across three lanes in traffic to get to the exit, but it's never too late to get off the highway and out of the herd.

Sometimes you are so far off course you don't even know if it is worth changing direction. The blue dot is so far away from where you thought it should be you feel like you might as well just stay on the highway. Just like any trip, the sooner you determine you are heading in the wrong direction, the quicker you can head in the right one. Finding who you really are and where your blue dot is will be the start.

Unlike the weekend road trip, in life the journey is everything.

It's the only thing.

Just like the Blue Goat zigging and zagging and changing direction, you will adjust and move where you are headed in life. It may be based on a feeling, insight from your co-pilot, or something you see that draws you to it. The key is that each of those choices are based one hundred percent on what you want to do, where you want to go, and the life you want to live. Once you pose the one true question, which is "What do I want out of my life?" then you realize that it doesn't matter what the herd is doing in the valley because the answer can only come from you.

Life is not a single event, or the arrival at a location, but the ongoing flow of each decision you make. Realizing that if we want something we've never had we may need to do something we've never done. Is your "life" the manifestation of you following the herd and getting the same results, or is it the realization of choosing your own path and finding the life you could only dream of? The fear we have so often along the journey is replaced by a much deeper fear when we come to the end and realize what wasn't. The life we didn't have, the joy we didn't feel, the love we missed.

Will you have a moment when you finally think to yourself "*I wish.*"

I wish I had quit that job.

I wish I laughed more.

I wish I had asked her out.

I wish I had lived abroad.

I wish I didn't take it all so seriously.

I wish I had spent more time with my kids.

Or will you look in the mirror and say, "*I did.*"

I did put myself first.

I did put myself out there and got rejected, but also found love.

I did see where I was and made the change to get to where I wanted to be.

I did fall on my face and have great failure, but I learned so much.

I freaking did it. I did my life. I wouldn't change a thing or wish for another shot at it.

The fears of getting dumped in your 20's, or losing the job in your 30's seem so small when you realize that the worry you had about those events are nothing compared to realizing too late that you let fear keep you from breaking out of the herd and living a life of your own. What changes should you make? What should you do differently? When the red pin drops, will you be exactly where you want to be?

What if that happened in two weeks, two months, two years? Will you be saying "*I wish*"?

A Blue Goat doesn't worry about the wilderness or let fear stand in the way of its life. Even with its hooves, it has figured out how to climb trees. When you realize what you are capable of, you understand that you can get off the paved road and navigate anything. Upon this realization of your unique gifts, skills, love, beauty and undeniable "Youness," you not only get off the highway but drive off road and begin to tread through the grass, over the rocks and chart your own course. Creating a path to a life that is as new, unique, and amazing as you are. With turns, twists and choices that only you could have.

You say, "*I did.*"

The assumed lack of options in our day-to-day lives can lead to a certain level of numbness to the opportunities we actually have. We think we can only drive on the highway with everyone else. It feels like the only option. We forget about the limitless possibilities when we choose our own path and blaze our own trail. You aren't stuck in your job. You aren't captive to the bad relationship. You aren't bound to your high mortgage and expensive cars. You can allow yourself to be if you want. We can make up every excuse and reason as to why things can't change, but that simply isn't reality. What you choose to believe determines the life you live.

You always have a choice. It's just a matter if you want to take it or not.

You can get a new job. You've done it before and you can do it again. You can break up and find a person who loves the one hundred percent you, instead of not really enjoying the eight-five percent version. You can change your lifestyle and not care at all about what others might think. You can live like no one is watching and no one is judging. You can do whatever you need to do.

You can.

Or you can seek out reasons why you can't.

Each moment where you don't honor your co-pilot and live your life is not just more time living in the herd, but months and years you are missing out on the limitless opportunities you truly have. The chance to explore your unique perspective, your innate gifts, and the ability to chart your own course, not for the purposes of standing out and drawing attention, but to honor your one shot at your life.

You can find yourself making decision after decision that weighs you down, saps your energy, drags down your vitality, or you can choose to find the moments, make the decisions, seek out the opportunities that give you goosebumps and create amazing energy that vibrates through your very being. The 'Blue Mist Moments'!

Thus, each moment in life is presented to you in a way to provide you with the opportunity to choose and craft your story.

Do you live your life like a sculptor? Do you chisel away the parts that you really don't need or the parts that aren't truly important to who you are? Do you see yourself as the amazing work of art that is hidden just below the surface? Have you looked at every aspect of your life to see that everything you keep is part of the greatest version of you? Do others get a say as to what is or isn't chiseled off, or do others come and add things to your sculpture that aren't what you want? Are you even the one holding the hammer and the sculpting tools, or have you given that over to someone else or society?

Such is your life. Your legacy is just as much a factor of what you keep in your life and even more so those aspects that you remove and don't serve a purpose for the piece of art you are creating. You can be the artist who looks at every aspect of the sculpture. See what edges need polishing, what aspects of the marble still need to be chipped away to leave behind the real version of who you are.

One of the scariest realities about life is that your last day will come and you will die.

For many, following what others are doing numbs that fear. We'd rather check the same boxes as the rest of the world, because then at least we are all in it together. Yet, with the right mindset we can live as if we have already had a chance at this life and made all the mistakes before.

You can imagine what you would think and feel if you made it to the end only to hear "Celebration" on the loudspeakers and see the "You Made it!" billboard on the horizon. You can imagine the disappointment, the sadness and the regret of what wasn't, what could have been, and all the life you left in the bottles.

Everything from the most impactful moments of the loss of a loved one to whether you react positively or negatively to the person who is rude to you at the checkout counter determines your future. You are truly self-determining because your attitude and decisions dictate the outcome of your life.

Your life is the most amazing gift you could ever ask for. You've won the lottery. It's just a matter of whether you want to cash in the ticket you hold in your hand. It's time to start asking yourself and the world around you why you are doing what you are doing.

You can choose to find the beauty in every moment, in every second and live for this time right now. Choose to be present and appreciate the gift of today, not constantly hoping for a better tomorrow. You can drink up life and leave nothing but empty water bottles in your wake.

You can allow yourself to find what moves you, what excites you and encourage your children to do the same.

You can create your own list for making your life the one you want and throw out the checkboxes you know won't bring you the true happiness you seek.

You can choose to do what you want and what you love. Find the things in life that make you come alive and encourage others to do the same.

You can realize that at the end you can look around at your life and say, "*This is it?*" Or you can realize this is the only life you have and say "*This is it!*"

You know that the world around you will throw so much at you. Without the right perspective, it can fundamentally change who you are. The world doesn't need the gunked-up angry version of you that is covered in garbage. You can let the trash go to the sewer where it belongs.

When choosing how to create the best version of your life, listen to yourself, find those intricate parts and talents and use them to create a recipe no one has ever seen before.

Realize that every second and each choice you are saying yes to someone and no to someone. Know how valuable you are and take ownership of what you do with your time. Find the balance between selfishness and being self-honoring by saying yes to you.

Listen, but to the right things. Drown out all the crap. Turn off the noise. Listen to the one person who is always looking out for you—your co-pilot.

Be fearful of the Golden Eggs. They are everywhere and are always being dangled in front of you as the goals you should be striving for. Choose where you want to go and what you want to strive for, not what others tell you to seek out.

Find the freedom in being you. Not the sixty-eight percent or eighty-three percent version. One hundred percent untouched and unfiltered you. The world will never know who you are if you hold anything back.

Remember the control you have over your decisions and choices. Each one truly matters and no one touches your dominos! Live with a purpose. BAM!

The filming will not stop until the last day of your life. Determine if the footage is of the movie you want your life to be. Change the plot, the scenery and everything else mid-movie if it totally sucks and is a dud so far. Surprise the hell out of everyone watching and make it become the best and most amazing come-from-behind story ever.

Choose to live and be you without the fear of what others will think. Make decisions because they honor you, not because it is what you think will impress others. Be the version that doesn't do things just to keep up with the other sheep.

Remember that each day you are getting closer to one of the two future versions of yourself. Choose wisely.

Look around to see the reality you have created and if it is your own, or one filled with news, posts, images, and information on the wall of the cave. Determine whose reality you should give your time to.

Realize that what you do and what you have isn't who you are. Your legacy will be so much more than that. People will remember how you made them feel far longer than what you had.

Cut ties with the past and release the pull of the future. Step out of the drain of replaying what was, let go of what might be. Find true peace and joy in being in the present.

Realize how truly powerful you are and how one degree of difference in your life can change everything.

It's time to finally become the unique snowflake everyone said you were. It's time to let the world know you are starting on a new road and beginning a new journey. To live with the understanding of what is really happening in the world around you. It's time to drive across three lanes of speeding traffic and maybe even piss others off on the way. It's time to pull off the highway and go off-roading and feel the grass and rocks under your car.

Sometimes the first step before we can find ourselves is realizing that we might be lost.

It's time to find yourself; it's time to find your blue dot.

How do you do that?

It's time to look in your own closet. To open all the drawers, cabinets and hiding places where you have been keeping the truth from yourself.

The truth about the life you have been living and more importantly the one you possibly haven't.

To look inward and be brutally honest about what you see.

To finally become comfortable in your own body and in your own life.

It starts with a new beginning.

I have this challenge for you.

To kick down the fence and step out into your new life.

Whatever it is that you find yourself posting on, scrolling through, or checking out daily turn away. Change your view. Adjust your perspective. Take time from looking at the screen and look in the mirror. Find out who is looking back. Take the time for you. Take the time to turn away from the cave and start to regain your relationship with your co-pilot and find exactly where your blue dot is.

Where are you in your life?

Who and what have you been measuring yourself against?

Are you who you want to be?

Where are you going?

Are you holding anything back?

Instead of standing in the bushes and peeking into others windows to see what they are doing, go back home and work on your own yard. Don't worry if your day or photo is Instagram worthy. Decide instead if it is worthy of you and the life you are creating. Remove the concern about whether someone else "likes" what you are doing and find the much more important answer which is do you "LOVE" what you are doing? Change from putting your curiosity and energy into the lives of those around you and finally put all your focus and energy into you.

It's time to show all your gifts with the world, all your talents and everything that you haven't shared yet. To shout from the rooftops and unleash your true untouched snowflake into the world around you. To live the life that has been waiting inside you this entire time. To find out what you want, what you love, and what isn't where it should be.

Post a single photo letting the world know you are starting a new journey and trying to figure out exactly where your blue dot is and where you want the next step to take you. That you are leaving the herd and charting your own course.

Share a photo of the Blue Goat, you holding this book, or whatever you feel tells everyone that you are no longer a sheep and from now on will be finding your own way. This will be the first step in you telling the world that you are setting out to find the most amazing life possible for yourself. Challenge yourself to spend at least one day off everything. Don't worry about what others are doing, what others are sharing, what advertisements you are being told you need.

When you want to login or go to the app just remember where you are putting your energy. For maybe the first time in a long time, you and your life deserve 100% of your focus. Nothing else does.

It's your time.

Time to be self-honoring. To look at all the intricate details of who you are and who you are capable of being. Take time for yourself. Turn off the flow of information that isn't for you.

Go off-road.

Spend time alone with a pen in your hand or your fingers on the keyboard with a blank page. Listen to yourself. Let your co-pilot talk and see what comes out. Allow you to show up. Just let it happen and see what you have to say. Listen to your thoughts and hear your inner dialogue. Go for a walk, relax on the couch, meditate, do what feels right.

Whatever post, article, news, or picture you will miss, you will gain so much more in finding where your blue dot is. Take the time to reflect. Take the time to think. Explore your emotions about where you are without the constant flow of what is going on with everyone else. Look at what you've been hiding in your own closet and start to clean off your own grate.

Challenge others to do the same, talk about life with your significant other, friends, ask your family about what matters to them. Begin new conversations about what is real. A true Blue Goat helps show the sheep that there is a way out of the pen and that they can escape too.

Start to rebuild the relationship with your co-pilot and begin anew.

It might be scary at first. You might miss all of it and be tempted to turn around and get back on the highway. When you start to feel it pulling at you, listen to the voice of your co-pilot. It will tell you exactly what you need to hear. In time, you might need to plug back into social media for certain things. Just pay attention to what it is you are plugging into.

You might need to follow new people to help you uncover different parts of yourself. You might need new teachers or to learn about opportunities for different experiences. Seek out, follow and explore the right things and the right people. See where they take you. Just remember that it is all about you and making your life everything you want it to be. You are finally starting to make your own recipe.

You are ready.

The bleating is getting louder.

The herd is growing bigger.

It's time.

Your time.

To finally become what you've been destined to be your entire life.

The most amazing version of you.

Go share your gifts with the world.

Live the life you only thought possible.

The World Needs You.

Be a Blue Goat.

BE YOU.

BLUE GOAT LIFE

This is my one life. The only one I will ever have. My actions are an outward expression of the incredible gift I know my life is. I value every moment and how I spend my time. I am filled with passion and purpose knowing that every decision will take me exactly where I need to be. I live each day without regret or the fear of failure.

I am amazing. I am a Blue Goat. I am me.

ABOUT THE AUTHOR

When I was a kid I wore a Superman cape everywhere I went. I felt like I had super powers and was capable of just about anything. On the jungle gym, I'd spread my arms wide holding my red cape in my outstretched hands. Over and over again I would jump, hoping one time it might just happen; that I would take off and fly.

Like so many before me, over time the cape came off and reality set in. I got older and school, then work, and the check boxes of what my life was supposed to be took over.

With time, I learned that so many others lost their capes and the sense of possibility along the way too.

So, this is me, climbing back up on the jungle gym.

Cape back on and arms spread wide.

I now know if I keep jumping, I'll always be flying.

For more about the author and Blue Goat Life explore www.bluegoatlife.com

Made in the USA
Columbia, SC
18 July 2018